GOOGLED BY GOD

GOOGLED BY GOD

...In Search of Money

Pulkit Ahuja

Srishti
PUBLISHERS & DISTRIBUTORS

Srishti Publishers & Distributors
Registered Office: N-16, C.R. Park
New Delhi – 110 019
Corporate Office: 212A, Peacock Lane
Shahpur Jat, New Delhi – 110 049
editorial@srishtipublishers.com

First published by
Srishti Publishers & Distributors in 2015

10 9 8 7 6 5 4 3 2 1

This is a work of fiction. The characters, places, organisations and events described in this book are either a work of the author's imagination or have been used fictitiously. All the technologies mentioned and described in this book either existed at the time of its writing or were being developed in a clandestine way.

Printed and bound in India

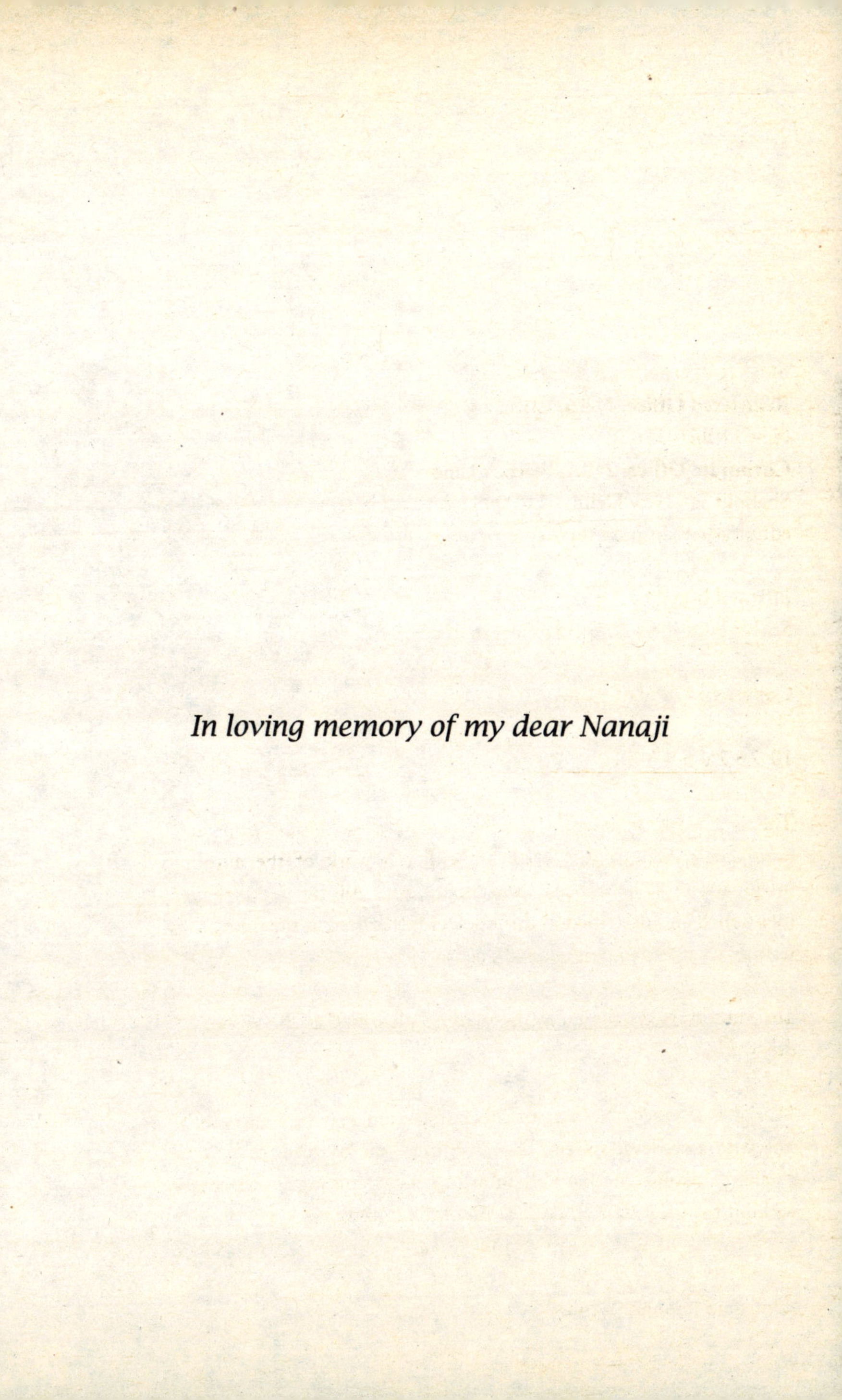

In loving memory of my dear Nanaji

Acknowledgements

A very big thanks to Mom, Dad and Bhai for their support and undying trust in my experiments. Without them, I would not have been possible.

A very big thanks to Abhijit Ghosh, Inderjit Singh Makkar, Lavanya Arora Sharma and all the wonderful folks at S&P Capital IQ, Gurgaon for nurturing an idea into being. Without them, this concept would not have been possible.

A special thanks to Nanima, Amit Chopra, Devan, Nehal Khosla, Sanchi Sethi and Vaibhav Tawakley for inspiring people around them to achieve bigger heights.

Last but not the least, a very big thanks to team Srishti for accepting and encouraging my writing. Without them, this book would not have been possible.

All the technologies mentioned and described in this book either existed at the time of its writing or were being developed in a clandestine way.

The Anomaly

DATE : THURSDAY, 1 JANUARY 2015

TIME : 1 A.M.

LOCATION : SOMEWHERE ON THE OUTSKIRTS OF DELHI

It was a dark room with the only source of light being a strip of bright blue LEDs which formed an oval on the ceiling. The LED strip extended from above the table on which an old outdated computer terminal flickered on one side of the room to the creaky door on the other side of the room.

The operator sitting next to the computer screen looked perplexed and worried, having no idea about whether to act on what he was seeing on the black terminal screen, or to dismiss it outright as a technical glitch. He would have opted for the latter had it not been for one of the two golden rules that he had learned in the past two years of his work at this place, ***'The Noek Never Errs'***.

On a usual day under normal circumstances, the screen would occasionally blurt out names of company stocks along with their suggested action - Buy or Sell. And this would not happen more than five or six times a day. Some days had even gone by when the operator kept staring at the screen for the entire day with nothing to show for his toil.

But this first day of the New Year was not turning out to be like any other usual day, and it seemed that the poor operator had no idea about the things that were to follow the chain of events that had been triggered as soon as the clock struck twelve and the entire nation started celebrating the New Year in their online and socially networked world.

The operator's gaze wandered over to the piece of paper that had been lying next to the screen since the past two years and then back to the black screen which was still flashing the same message in red:

STOCK	CODE	RECOMMENDATION
SAHIL KASHYAP	008751347852	BUY

This was a situation that required action and something needed to be done fast. Time was of essence and the young operator's instructions were crystal clear when he had been hired for this job –

He was to maintain no contact with the outside world; no vacations, and no leaving the terminal unattended by abandoning the room. He was to deliver the stocks' name as soon as it flashed on the terminal along with its suggested action.

At first, these instructions had seemed pretty strange to young Jatin when they were laid down to him during the interview. To find out if it was a prank by his crazy friends, he had decided to play along. But the compensation package which included a joining bonus of twenty-five lakh rupees deposited in advance to an overseas account in his name removed this and any other such doubts that Jatin might have had about the seriousness of the offer.

So much money for such a simple job! Are these people crazy? he had said to himself. What Jatin had not realised at the time of accepting the offer was that he would be virtually disappearing from the face of the earth for the time he would be the operator. No questions asked.

But even then, one thing that the balding man with a strong Russian accent had not told Jatin when he hired him was - what was Jatin supposed to do if the name on the screen was no longer a stock but a real person?

It was 1.15 a.m. already and the terminal screen was still repeatedly blinking the same message after every couple of minutes.

Jatin's eyes glanced over to the paper again and again, unable to decide whether or not he should make the call. He decided that it was time to follow the second golden rule blindly, 'Whenever the Noek delivers a name, you make the call.'

Without further ado, for the first time in his tenure as the operator, Jatin grabbed the second of the two phones lying in front of him and dialled the number which had the warning next to it…

The phone was answered after a single ring and Jatin started, "I think you should see this —"

root id - admin

password - shark@8e4mas

In case of Emergency Only - +7 7858652124

One Time Use

He was interrupted before he could say anything further by a baritone voice he had never heard before, and the reply could not have been more precise –

"We know."

Beep, beep, beep!

And the call was disconnected.

Round Two

Price is what you pay. Value is what you get.

—Warren Buffet

ONE YEAR AGO, 1 JANUARY 2014

It was an ethereal winter day, with light warm sunshine and cool winds. A happy day for people at the office of Pay-kwik Technologies. It was a day when at least two BMWs would be booked by the two co-founders of Pay-kwik. After all, they had just sold a minority stake of their company to JONAS Partners for a whopping fifty million dollars.

JONAS Partners was led by Akram, a dominating and go-for-the-kill kind of person who had little regard for anything that could not be expressed in terms of a pile of money. Akram had joined JONAS as a fresher straight out of Narsee Monjee College of Commerce and Economics, when JONAS Partners was just a five member team situated in a suburban Andheri West office. And over a span of fifteen years, through his intelligence coupled with his ruthless aggression and little regard for rules, Akram had literally propelled JONAS to become one of the biggest names in the Indian investment industry. It now had more than two hundred employees in five offices spread across the country.

There was commotion all around at the Noida office of Pay-kwik as the announcement that JONAS has invested fifty million dollars in their company for an equity stake of thirty percent in the second round of funding was made public. This New Year had brought with it new dimensions for Pay-kwik.

Pay-kwik Technologies had started as an online service provider for easy mobile recharges, which enabled customers to quickly make their mobile top-up payments online, thereby the name Pay-kwik. Initially with Pay-kwik, customers could get their mobile recharges done from the convenience of their homes as well. But as competition increased and margins decreased over time, the company had also started selling deals and products on their website, and then finally moved on to develop India's first virtual wallet.

Pay-kwik's virtual wallet was one of the very few wallets available to the Indian user which were approved by the RBI to hold users' money virtually, enabling them to pay without the hassle of logging into their bank accounts every time they wanted to spend online. And with JONAS Partners buying a 30% stake in it for fifty million dollars, the net valuation of the company had crossed a gigantic 160 million dollars; one thousand crore rupees of company valuation after just round two[(1)] of its funding.

From mobile recharges to almost becoming a virtual bank, from Rupees zero to Rupees one thousand crores, the past three years had been a crazy journey for this start-up.

There were balloons and confetti all around the office alleys and seats. It seemed as if every employee of this hundred employee company was having their birthday on the same day. And why shouldn't it be so – a company like Pay-kwik which was started by the two co-founders from a small flat, had today etched itself in the Indian start-up history forever by raising approximately half a million dollars per employee. There was nowhere to go from here but up, especially with one of the biggest names in the investment industry now backing Pay-kwik.

The documents had been signed the previous evening and the money would be transferred to the co-founder's accounts and the company account shortly. The earlier investors, Prime Venture Fund, had made a successful exit earning a total return of 800% on their first round of funding in Pay-kwik Technologies.

A part of the money was to go to the Prime Venture Fund for their forfeiture of the company holdings, a second part to the co-founders for their dilution of founders stock as a secondary offering and the rest into company account as an investment.

"Congratulations on the successful completion of the deal, Akram," said Mukul clinking his wine glass with Akram's at the central gathering.

"Cheers to you too!" said Akram raising his wine glass.

Mukul was the lead analyst at JONAS Partners who looked into ventures of Financial Technology domain. He had researched, proposed and carried out the nitty-gritties of the investment proposal groundwork for Pay-kwik on behalf of JONAS.

"Cheers!" replied Mukul with a beaming smile while raising a toast to Akram.

3 Fs

Sometimes, your best investments are the ones you don't make.

—Donald Trump

THREE WEEKS LATER AT JONAS' OFFICE, GURGAON
21 JANUARY 2014

It was a silent day with everyone seeming busy with their own work. The receptionist, a fair lady with dark golden-brown hair and pout lips was the only person sitting in clear view of Rahul, who was waiting on one of the three sofas that formed the waiting area of this office. *Such a small waiting area meant that not many people made it there and he must be one of the lucky few,* thought Rahul to himself.

Rahul had a business plan (B-Plan)[(2)] for which he was trying to raise seed funding. Considering that less than one percent of start-ups ever raise venture capital funding, Rahul had already tried his hands on approaching the First 3 Fs of funding: Friends, Family and Fools. But like most, he had failed miserably at convincing any of them about his own ability to bring to life the flowery words he had written in his B-Plan.

And now there he was, lost in his thoughts while sitting on that comfortable reception sofa and waiting to meet with the

JONAS Analyst who Rahul had been introduced to over a mail and who looked into Financial Technology related B-Plans for JONAS.

"This kind of an ambitious project would need at least five crores as starting capital," Rahul's brother, who worked as an assistant professor of Finance had told Rahul from his past experience in the industry,

To which Rahul's reply had been, "No, I can start this business with much less. I have already applied for a patent on this technology, which will ensure I have no other competitors for the next seventeen years."

"You'd still need at least a couple of crores as initial investment for establishing the basic infrastructure for such a technology to work. And neither dad nor I have that kind of money, bro," his brother had replied. And there was lost Rahul's First F of funding – the Family.

But, surprisingly his best friends (the second F) had been much more enthusiastic about his venture plans.

Rahul had met them at his rented flat on the New Year's Eve to discuss his plan. His wolf pack consisted of Shiva, Arjun and Ankit – his three best friends for life that he had made during his three years at the Hindu College, Delhi University. The four of them were famous throughout the college as an epitome of friendship. Brothers for life they called themselves; *All for One and One for All* was their motto.

"Wow bro, this is such a good idea," Shiva said when the four of them met.

"Yeah exactly, this is it... the next biiiiig thingggg," a drunk Arjun shouted.

"Seriously Rahul, that's a great idea. Tell us what you need from us and we will do our best," a sober Ankit suggested.

"Buddies, I need capital and manpower. Money that I can spend to get the various aspects of the technology going and people that I can trust to spend that money wisely," Rahul demanded. "And from you my friends, I ask for both."

There was a long silence at Rahul's flat before Ankit finally spoke, "How much are we talking about?"

"At least a couple of crores," was Rahul's reply.

"What?" Arjun shouted while spitting out the vodka that was still in his mouth. He was fully back to his senses after Rahul's shocking demand.

But Arjun was not the only one shocked. Shiva had gone mum.

Ankit replied, "But there is no way we three can shell out that kind of money buddy, even if we ask our parents. They would not give us more than a few lakhs."

"Why don't you ask Natasha?" Ankit suggested referring to Rahul's love interest who also happened to be the daughter of a very influential man.

"Yes, why don't you ask bhabhi? She would surely be able to help," Shiva finally spoke.

All three of them referred to Natasha as their bhabhi as they were sure both Rahul and Natasha were not going to love anyone else but each other their entire lives. Although they had not proposed to each other yet, everyone who was close to either Rahul or Natasha knew whose name it would be on the invitation cards they'd receive.

"You know I would never do that," Rahul replied. And not surprisingly, each one of them knew that he never would, considering his self-respect.

All of them were back to square one, and there went Rahul's second F of funding – the Friends.

"Buddy, I have a friend whose brother works in one of these big shot investment firms. They make insane amounts of investments in these new technology businesses. And with a plan as awesome as yours, I am sure they would give you all the money you need in the world," Ankit spoke after a lot of thought.

Suddenly there was a ray of hope, maybe the last one for Rahul. It took no time for Rahul to grab it.

"Sure man. That would be wonderful," Rahul replied.

"Cool, will ask my friend's brother to introduce you to the concerned guy over email. And then once you meet him and have the funding, you can hire us all to work under you," Arjun said beaming from ear to ear as he made his drink.

"You will be the last ones who I would have working under me, buddies. If we pull this off, we all will be working together in the morning and enjoying the high life by the evening," Rahul replied, more to himself than anyone else in the room.

Rahul's thoughts were interrupted when his name was called out by the receptionist for the second time.

"Mr Rahul," she said placing back a few strands of her hair which had come loose from behind her right ear. "Mr. Mukul, who deals with technology investment proposals for the firm had to go out for an emergency meeting. He has asked you to submit your plan with me, and told me to let you know that he will surely get back to you if he finds your proposal worthy of his time and company's investment," the receptionist concluded.

Rahul hesitated a bit, the brown leather file containing the physical copy of the B-Plan clenched tightly in his hands, *Should I hand over my hard worked projections, industry study, proof of concept, survey reports and my idea to this unknown damsel?* he thought to himself.

His thoughts were interrupted for a second time by the receptionist's question. "Mr Rahul, would you like to submit the same now or would you like to come back some other time?" she said, the 'come back some other time' just being a nicer way of saying 'you might not get a second chance'.

Rahul stood up and walked up to the receptionist.

And in a moment of desperation, he decided that this might be his last opportunity in the foreseeable future to gain a funding for his idea and convert it into a start-up,

"Fuck it. I own the patent to this technology, and worse comes to worst, someone can only steal my idea, not my patent," he said to himself. and handed over the hundred-page file to the beautiful receptionist.

Dad's Treat

Ah! There is nothing like staying at home, for real comfort.
—Jane Austen

It was 7.58 p.m. When the door key clicked, his dad knew that Sahil was back home. The hall of the 2 BHK flat that Sahil had rented for himself and his dad was a mixture of the old and the new. The movable furniture was mostly cane, while the fixed wooden cupboards that the good old landlady had got made at the time of the construction of the flat were made of plywood coated with sunmica. The kitchen hardly had any room for more than two people to stand side by side and not touch shoulders, so the fridge had to be adjusted into the hall along with the common 29 inch television and the only window AC in the house.

Sahil kept his office bag on the single seater cane sofa next to the one on which his dad was pretending to be asleep. The television was on and tuned into one of the business news channels. Sahil's laptop was logged into and the lights were all turned on – ideal conditions for his dad to do whatever he used to do during the day.

"Dad, did the maid not come today?" Sahil called out as he entered the kitchen. Utensils from the previous day lay unwashed in the sink and there was no food that had been cooked earlier in the day.

There was no reply from his dad, who was still busy pretending to be asleep,

"Dad," shouted Sahil, "C'mon I know that you are not sleeping. Turn off the television and tell me what should I cook for dinner?" Sahil asked.

His dad opened his left eye, then his right and answered slowly trying to sound sleepy. "You don't need to cook, beta. I have already ordered pizzas for both of us. They said they would deliver in half an hour's time."

"Dad, you are such a sweetheart. You know that now, don't you," said Sahil coming out of the kitchen and sitting next to him.

"Yes, I know, and now you better go and change, while I wrap up my work," his dad responded patting Sahil's head.

Sahil would have tried to ask what work he was doing, but he already knew the answer. He had asked this question a thousand times, and a thousand times his dad had replied, "Nothing much, beta, just a few searches and a study of what's going on in the outside world."

Sahil had not tried to play detective as he was happy that at least his dad was keeping himself occupied, especially because his dad hadn't had a job for as long as Sahil could remember. The two BHK flat could get very lonely for a person staying alone at home during the major part of the day, but apparently his dad liked it that way. Solitude is what he sought. His dad had even tried to convince Sahil that he could himself manage the daily chores and they should get rid of the maid as well.

"She is such a disturbance, always chit chatting about one thing or the other during the entire time she is in the house," was his justification of why they should fire her.

To which Sahil's response had always been constant, "Dad, you need to get used to company. I will get married soon."

That 'will soon get married', however, had not come in the past few years.

Mr Kashyap had been in prison for some years when Sahil was young, and Sahil's mom had often told him tales of how his time in prison had changed Mr Kashyap completely. "Your father used to be a very trusting, socialising and cheerful man," she used to say, to which Sahil used to ask, "But why was dad in prison?"

Sahil never got a straight reply for this question.

"There are things that you won't understand," Sahil's mother had said. "There were some complications and then he was sent to prison and banned from trading in the stock markets forever."

That was all that he had been able to get out of her mother.

And now that his mother was no more, there was no one who could have told Sahil what had really been the reason.

Ever since his father had moved in with Sahil after his mother's demise, Sahil had never seen any of his dad's friends come to visit him. He even doubted that his dad had any friends that he still spoke to.

The bell rang at the front door and by the time Sahil came out of the washroom, his dad had already paid for the pizzas and put them on the centre cane table.

A sumptuous dinner was on the cards.

"We should have called over your brother as well; it's been a week I have not seen him. He called up yesterday and said he would not be coming over this weekend as well. He has to go out of town on company work," said Mr Kashyap.

"Dad, the traffic's terrible. It'll take him more than two hours to get here. Let us just have the pizzas and then you can go to sleep," replied Sahil.

After dinner, Sahil thanked his dad for the lovely treat and recited the same lines which he had grown accustomed to saying since the last few years. "Dad, in case you need money or anything, please let me know."

To which, he received the same practiced answer which he had been hearing from his dad,

"No son, I am good. But if you need or want anything, just say it and I will get it for you. Whatever I have gathered over the years anyways belongs to you and your brother," he replied. "Whether you ask for it now or I gift it to you at the time of my death is just a matter of time."

"Yes Dad, I know, and please stop talking like that. I will tell you if there is anything I need, thank you. Now sleep well, good night," said Sahil while accompanying Mr Kashyap to his room.

Loaded Shells

Honesty is the best policy - when there is money in it.

—Mark Twain

STOCK	CODE	RECOMMENDATION
APOLLO TYRES	APT	STRONG BUY

Jatin glanced at the machine's latest prediction on the terminal screen and picked up the attached landline phone to dial the next phone number in his ledger list.

The phone number was attributed to Orini Traders, one of the numerous shell corporations belonging to the PAN Group of Companies, the company which owned the Noek.

"Stock Name - Apollo Tyres, Bombay Stock Exchange Code - APT, Buy Aggressively. Target you have left for this month is rupees three crores. Statutory update - to avoid being red flagged by the regulators, at no point should your earnings for the remaining days in this financial year exceed rupees fifteen crores," announced Jatin on the phone as soon as it was picked on the other side.

"Message received. Please confirm trade - Apollo Tyres, APT, Aggressive Buy call, suggested profit to be booked till month end is rupees three crores, maximum remaining profit to be booked for the financial year is rupees fifteen crores," repeated a voice on the other side.

"Confirmed," said Jatin and disconnected the phone. He was one down for the day. That is all Jatin was required to do each day to ensure his daily pay of one lakh rupees got into his overseas bank account.

This was a typical day for Jatin at this one-man office of the PAN Group of Companies, a multinational company that had Russian roots and was listed in the National Stock Exchange as a public limited company.

It had been almost a year since Jatin had joined PAN group in February 2013, and he had been earning a lakh each day for doing what he just did, over and over again every time the machine came up with a new stock suggestion which was then displayed to Jatin on the old and outdated terminal screen. There was no fixed count of the number of stock predictions that could come from the Noek each day, but during Jatin's stay, the number of predictions had typically been between five to six stocks per day. The only other thing that differed for Jatin every time there was a new prediction was the shell company that he had to pick from the ledger list and call to forward the machine's stock predictions.

When Jatin accepted the job of being the machine's operator, apart from the strange instructions about no holidays and no contact with the outside world, the Russian guy who had recruited him gave him a list he referred to as the ledger list. The ledger list contained the names and contact numbers of several shell companies, companies that had existed only on paper with no real operations and which belonged to the PAN Group of Companies.

The PAN Group had created these large number of shell companies to prevent their abnormally high profits in the stock markets from being investigated by any regulatory authority. PAN had been earning such profits since the past several years on account of the Noek's predictions, and dividing that kind of money among a huge number of dummy companies made it look less suspicious than putting all of it in a single company's account.

And Jatin's job was to ensure that the profits from these predictions were booked by the shell companies in an appropriate and uniform way, hence avoiding the possibility of even one of them making huge profits and leading to exposing itself and the other shells. The errorless execution of this delicate mechanism had ensured that the presence of such a machine which was capable of making abnormal profits by predicting the stock market movements remained a secret. The century's best kept secret about Indian stock markets.

Only two people in the world knew how this entire system worked, all others who were privy of this knowledge were either dead or had gone missing over the past several years.

Jatin's knowledge about this process was limited to him receiving stock names and their suggested actions from a machine terminal, information which he was made to believe was sent from an overseas group of phenomenal stock market analysts who used artificial intelligence and called themselves 'The Noek'.

Funny name for a group of analysts he had thought. "Sounds more like a name for a rock band," was Jatin's first candid comment in front of Frank when he was being briefed by Frank about his role as the Operator.

While the traders of the shell companies who received orders from Jatin were also under a similar impression, there were two major differences. One major difference was that these employees of PAN were one step lower in the hierarchy of information flow and therefore the pay scale. And for them, Jatin, the guy who called them, was the analyst predicting the trades.

The second major difference was that the employees working as a part of any one shell company office were unaware of the existence of several other such companies under the PAN umbrella.

The common point between Jatin and the people working in these shell companies was that all of them were paid well enough to not think about why and how were all the stock predictions that they received always correct.

The only two people who actually knew about whole process were the Founder and CEO of the PAN Group of Companies and his most trusted aide, Frank - the balding man with the Russian accent who had recruited Jatin.

Frank had just one job: to ensure that the PAN group of companies continued making their profits on account of Noek's continued and uninterrupted clandestine operations.

And the reason that the existence of Noek remained PAN group's best kept secret was largely because of the fact that Frank was very good at his job of doing all the dirty work.

Frank was responsible for making sure that his boss's hands and image remained clean.

False Truths

In the time of universal deceit – telling the truth is a revolutionary act.

—George Orwell

After going through the entire file twice, Mukul had little doubt that they would have to necessarily invest in Rahul's B-Plan proposal. *They had to invest, there was no escaping it,* Mukul thought to himself.

And this time around, it was not the greed of making money from an investment that had so desperately convinced Mukul about his disposition, but rather it was the fear of losing all the money that they had already invested in Pay-kwik that was at the root of Mukul's utter desperation. JONAS's four week old fifty-million dollar investment was at the risk of soon becoming zero because of what Rahul had left on those pages in his file.

With JONAS aggressively backing Pay-kwik, a company working towards putting their own custom-made online wallet in every user's pocket through their smartphones, any new technology that made the need of such wallets redundant without changing the user behaviour was a mortal threat to Pay-kwik's business model and thus JONAS's investment.

These threats were not uncommon to Mukul considering his involvement in technology related ventures. "Our technology changes faster than you change your girlfriends," Mukul had once said on stage while addressing a teenage audience when he was invited to give a guest lecture by his alma mater.

In the past, whenever Mukul and JONAS were faced with such a threat, they always had an exit option ready to liquidate their investments by selling off their stakes to a greater fool[3] if the path ahead started to seem tough. And in case they were unable to find a greater fool than themselves, they used to improvise and have the company that they invested in to copy an upcoming and promising idea. And with their vast resources and already existing setup, JONAS ensured that they spread this new product or service in the market much before the upcoming competitor with the original idea got any time to acquire some significant market share.

But, in the current case, both these options had somehow been nullified. They could not find any investor just four weeks into their investment in a start-up for which they themselves negotiated for investor exclusivity rights. Even a casual talk of JONAS's disinvestment from Pay-kwik would lead to a diminishing market confidence in Pay-kwik.

While on the other hand, Mukul or Akram could not have deployed their strong handing techniques to force Pay-kwik into copying Rahul's technology. This was because of the very reason that Rahul had handed over his file to the receptionist - Rahul already held a patent and hence the exclusive rights for developing and using this technology.

As soon as Mukul kept the file back on the desk, he rushed to his intercom and dialled 311 - the code for Akram's office.

"Akram, you need to see this now," was all that Mukul said in a voice as grave as the expression on his face.

Ⓑ

Akram shortly called a meeting with Mukul in his cabin to investigate further into the perceived threat that Mukul had approached Akram with.

Had it been just another day, Akram would have laughed Mukul's fears off like any one of those hundreds of wannabe business plans that were passed to him on a daily basis by his team of analysts, claiming those B-Plans to be probable investments of interest. All of those ended up in Akram's recycle bin by the same evening.

But today, Mukul sounded as though he had seen a ghost in that file – a ghost that was rearing its threatening head out of the file and directly at JONAS Partners' balance sheet.

Akram had asked Mukul to prepare a detailed analysis of the Whats, What Ifs, Hows and Whens of the perceived threat and its suggested counter measures.

As the meeting started, Mukul assumed the speaker's part with his presentation containing an in-depth analysis of how badly a product like Rahul's proposed 'Universal Card' could impact JONAS's latest investment of buying a stake in Pay-kwik.

The concept of 'Universal Card' or 'uCard' as Rahul had put it in his file, was aimed at developing a single universal payment system which would fit in the size of a regular credit card physically but would have the ability to be connected 24*7 with any and all the online accounts and virtual wallets of the user. So the users would be able to swipe the card just like a normal credit or debit card and shop physically using the balance in their accounts across various banks and online wallets.

This was the less worrying part for JONAS and Pay-kwik's business model; the more worrying part however was that the card was proposed to provide a reverse compatibility as well. That meant that the users would be able to shop online without the need of having a bank account with net banking facilities, a real credit/debit card or even a virtual wallet. The uCard's number was supposed to work on all websites as well just like a normal credit/debit card number.

The card was proposed to be linked directly to the user's several bank accounts so that they could complete any transaction using combined balances from all their bank accounts that they had linked with their uCard.

While Pay-kwik was working on putting their own virtual wallet in the users' pockets through the route of their mobile phones, Rahul's technology could completely change the game. The uCard had the potential to rise across all boundaries that existed in this domain by providing a single acceptable solution without impacting user behaviour. Just one card that could be used online as well as offline, and which could be linked with real bank accounts as well as virtual wallets. All this in the size of a regular credit card. The uCard was designed to integrate everything that a user would ever need.

Pay-kwik and JONAS were finding themselves caught in the wildfire of disruptive technology.

After the presentation ended, it was clear to Akram that this was an idea that was much ahead of its time, and when its time came, JONAS needed to be on the right side of the table.

Akram realised that this technology needed to be owned, but there was something else which was bothering Akram a lot more. It was not just the investment, but the timing. If they were to invest in Rahul's idea and rush it to the market, they would be jeopardising and cannibalising their latest investment in Pay-kwik, which Akram had vouched for personally. But at the same time, they could not let Rahul continue his search for investors in the market and risk the idea being picked up by any of their competitors.

"We need to own this," murmured Akram to himself lost in his own thoughts.

"What options do we have?" Akram straightened up and asked Mukul.

"If we do not fund him and he is unable to raise investments from any other investor as well, it might take him a very long time to bring his plan into existence. It at present anyway seems farfetched. By that time, we might be able to exit our Pay-kwik investment, booking some profits over the period of the next two to three years," answered Mukul.

"But are we ready to take such a huge gamble of letting this boy approach any other investor with a copy of his plan?" argued Akram.

"Any good analyst worth his salt would recognize the potential that Rahul's plan has and they might not take very long to fund him and help him launch this product," replied Mukul.

Akram went back to his thoughts after listening to Mukul's replies.

"Mukul, please follow up with this entrepreneur of yours and arrange a one to one meeting with him this Wednesday at our office," demanded Akram after giving it a lot of thought.

This was the strangest thing Mukul had heard Akram demand since he had started working for JONAS Partners. Akram was one of those who was at the top of their game and strongly believed in the power of hierarchy. He was the one who propagated the notion that things needed to be earned, himself creating stiff competition for anyone soliciting for his time and attention.

On his way out of Akram's office, Mukul approached Akram against his better sense and asked him what the hell he was thinking in the politest of the ways known to him.

"Akram, I don't suppose you meeting with a potential investment seeker so early in the negotiations will be an apt step as far as the dynamics of negotiations are concerned. Let me follow up with him over a couple of weeks and then maybe we can set up a meeting for both of you to meet," Mukul said.

Akram looked at Mukul in amusement as though he had not heard a single word of what Mukul had said and replied, "When you are in front of a moving train, what you need is speed and a sense of direction, not a strategy to save yourself. No matter how apt a strategy you apply, if you don't move fast enough, you will get crushed."

Rahul came in fifteen minutes before time and was waiting on the same sofa in JONAS's waiting area for the second time in a span of two weeks.

"Mr Rahul, please follow me. Akram will meet you now," said the same receptionist, who two weeks ago had told Rahul to come back at a later time.

Rahul got up from his sofa and followed the fair lady into one of the corner rooms. This particular corner room was a small one with a round table to seat a maximum of four people. This meant that not many people would be present to interview and grill Rahul on his financial projections and cost estimates during this meeting. The thought brought a smile to Rahul's face.

Akram walked into the room two minutes after Rahul made himself comfortable at the round table and was served water by one of the pantry boys.

"Good evening," said Akram with a straight face.

"Good evening," replied Rahul with a smile.

Akram was carrying Rahul's file which he had left with the receptionist during his last visit to this office. He opened his file while he sat down on a seat opposite Rahul's across the table.

"So Mr Rahul, firstly I would like to ask you about how many investors have you approached till now or have sent this plan to. And be very frank with me for the benefit of both of us," Akram said going straight to the point, skipping any small talk.

"Sir, JONAS is the first firm that I have approached with this plan. Before this, I tried explaining this plan to a group of my friends and my brother, but they didn't understand much of it," replied Rahul, slightly nervous.

"Okay, then we are good to proceed," replied Akram with a sigh of relief.

"So I will come directly to the point without wasting much of your time or mine," Akram began the negotiations in a stern tone. "In your plan you have written that you need to raise five crores as seed funding and you are willing to give away 33% of the company's shares," Akram continued.

"Yes sir," replied Rahul, matter of factly.

"So this puts the net value of the company at rupees fifteen crores for 100% shares," said Akram.

"Yes sir," Rahul replied again, not sure as to exactly where the conversation was headed.

"And according to your estimates, the execution of this technology would need at least six to eight months of development time and then extremely hard labour for its marketing," said Akram.

"Yes sir, and I am looking forward to this hard work and extensive learning involved during the process," replied Rahul, finally saying something apart from his two-word answers which had remained constant for all of Akram's questions.

"And what are your expectations and exit plans from this business? What are the returns that you are targeting?" Akram finally asked a question that was not in Rahul's file.

"I am not looking to exit this business, sir. It is my dream and I would like to keep growing it as much as possible," replied Rahul taken a bit off-guard by Akram's first real question since the meeting had started.

There was a sly smile on Akram's face as though he was mocking Rahul for his naivety.

"These idealistic answers are fine but you and I both know that none of us are here to marry this business. So there must be a figure in your mind you aim to achieve if this venture becomes successful?" Akram asked after a short pause, the sly smile still on his face.

"No sir, I haven't. And I won't like to leave it after putting in so much hard work to set it up," came an earnest reply from Rahul.

Akram had gauged that the conversation was going nowhere and so he thought of trying a different strategy - a strategy that involved a more direct approach.

"Let me be very frank with you, Rahul. What if I tell you that you don't even have to put yourself through all that hard work, wait for so long and then pray that the venture is a success to make that kind of money," said Akram, his pitch rising.

"Name a price. You say fifteen crores is a fair worth but that involves a very long wait, very long hours at work and then the uncertainty of the idea becoming a success among the masses," Akram continued. "I offer you twenty crores right now. Take it and walk away from this B-Plan. Transfer your patent and other intellectual property rights related to this idea to JONAS. Pick up another idea. Million dollar ideas are dime a dozen. Make your next idea your dream and you will have enough money of your own to invest in your next many ventures," Akram said finally, dropping the bombshell on Rahul.

"I did not get what you are trying to say, sir," Rahul replied confused. He must have misunderstood what Akram was trying to tell him, Rahul felt.

"JONAS wants to buy 100% equity in this venture and along with it, all your intellectual property rights and patents for a flat out payment," replied Akram in clear, concise terms.

"But what do you plan to do with it? No one can work on my idea better than me, so why think of excluding me?" asked an even more confused Rahul after hearing Akram's proposal.

"Don't get me wrong, Rahul. Your plan is an ambitious one, but at the same time, it is a little too early for a market as nascent as India to accept this technology easily and without scepticism about how safe this card is," replied Akram. "We believe that the right time to launch a product like the uCard in the Indian markets would be around three or four years down the line, and we don't want you to wait for so long to start earning your profits. Keeping that in mind, we have decided that we would be happy to buy your plan at a flat down payment and launch the uCard in the Indian markets when the time is right," Akram concluded with a smile.

Rahul was left baffled and his expressions were not helping in hiding the fact. It seemed as if the floor beneath his feet had been swept away by Akram.

"Oh c'mon Rahul, let us not get all sentimental about it and let's start thinking of it from a practical view point. It's a business, after all. Perhaps one of the many you will be doing in your life ahead," Akram added looking at Rahul's expression.

At this point, Rahul was clearly starting to understand what JONAS was trying to conspire.

"I came here to get an investment for an idea that is my dream and my baby. It is not about the money for me, but about creating something that will be remembered forever. In case you are mistaken, I am not here to sell you some fancy wine at an auction that you will bid for and not use for three years," exclaimed Rahul unable to control his rage.

"That's good enough for us then," said Akram closing Rahul's file and keeping it on the round table. "It's a deal."

"I don't think you got me," replied Rahul. "I would not like to take the deal. Thank you for your time, and can I please have my file back?" Rahul urged.

"Relax, child," Akram spoke in a much calmer tone this time. "I heard you clearly."

"It was a test to see whether you are in it for the real thing or just the money," continued Akram with a smile.

"Ninety-nine percent people would have opted for the money, and they would have gotten neither the money for themselves, nor the investment from JONAS," Akram winked.

"And I dare say that you are one of the very few who passed this test with flying colours. Congratulations, Mr Rahul, we would like to invest five crore rupees in your venture," announced Akram, picking up Rahul's file again.

The Day we Flew

When love is not madness it is not love.

—Pedro Calderón de la Barca

After Rahul and Natasha had graduated from Hindu College, Rahul had always thought of asking Natasha to marry him, but could never gather the courage to do so. He wanted it to be an event of a lifetime, to make it as special as it could get.

"When I propose to Natasha, it would be a story we'd tell our grandkids," he used to joke with his friends.

That evening on his way back home from JONAS's office, Rahul decided that he should celebrate the good news of his B-Plan getting seed funded in a grand way by proposing to the love of his life. He started going over scenarios of how he could make it special for the girl who already had everything.

As soon as he reached his one BHK rented flat in Cyber City, he logged on to Expedia and started using his imagination in designing a dream weekend getaway. At six the following Saturday morning, Rahul had a limousine waiting at his door, technically waiting at the end of his street as the driver called him up and insisted there was no way he could bring the limo into his street without getting it scratched on both sides courtesy the parked two wheelers and cars on both sides of the ten-feet wide society road.

He settled himself inside the limo and asked the driver to take him to Natasha's place in the posh Sunder Nagar society on their way to the airport. The roads were empty at this hour in the morning and Rahul could see the sun slowly come out of trees as they crossed Lodi Gardens on the left, which had woken up to the capital's most influential people jogging around in their tracksuits, some alone and others with their pets across the rich green contour settled amid a scenic medieval heritage fort. Rahul suddenly felt that he had changed his breed and had joined the rich and affluent right in their home ground. It was a new dawn with a wonderful view of the sunrise.

Natasha was the only daughter of the Director General of Telecommunications, Mr Sethi, and had known Rahul since her first year of Stats Honours in Hindu College, Delhi University. Since the first day that they had met, Rahul had often wondered about what exactly Natasha saw in him, considering she was a college superstar with a fan following enough to humble even the DUSU election candidates. He on the other hand was an average teenager with just enough friends to keep him from getting bored to death during the college lectures.

Natasha took around ten minutes to come out of her bungalow after Rahul reached. However, seeing Natasha come out at 6:30 a.m. was like witnessing a second sunrise within a gap of thirty minutes. It seemed like the days were surely changing for Rahul, and good days had arrived.

Natasha was wearing a knee length bright yellow dress with white four-inch wedges and a long silver necklace to compliment her silver Gucci watch with a white dial and intermittent white pearls on its bracelet. And as if her clothes were not enough to blow Rahul off his feet that morning, Natasha in anticipation of the day ahead had decided to put on a bit of eye makeup - a tinge of kajal and silver eyeliner. Her eyes occasionally hidden by her perfectly straight hair seemed to be casting a magical spell on Rahul as she crossed her parking area towards the waiting limo.

Once she got into the car and the chauffeur took off for the airport, Rahul was still having difficulty adjusting to the new Natasha. All he was privy to was the cowboy-like girl dressed in jeans and a t-shirt with a pair of shades hanging around her neck.

"Ahem, ahem… Rahul! You are staring," she said, wearing the same shy smile that had so enchanted Rahul the first time they had met.

"I what? Oh, am so sorry," said Rahul, a bit embarrassed.

"Why sorry? You can stare. I am not looking that bad, am I?" Natasha replied with a wink.

"No my angel, you are the most beautiful sunrise I have ever seen in my life," blushed Rahul, his cheeks turning red as he continued talking to her.

"And by the way, mister, nice car. When did you buy it? You didn't even bother telling me, huh!" Natasha teased him.

Once they reached the domestic terminal at the Delhi airport, the chauffeur handed them their business class tickets for their flight to Jaipur.

In the flight, Natasha was still surprised as to how Rahul had planned everything without letting her get a whiff of what was in store for the day. She was taken by surprise when Rahul had called her up a couple of days back and asked her if she would be free the coming Saturday and had requested her to be ready at six in the morning.

Her thoughts were interrupted by the announcement on the flight which told them that the temperature outside was a pleasant twenty-four degree Celsius with clouds covering major portions of the blue sky. As the two of them exited the Jaipur airport, Natasha spotted a chauffeur holding a placard with the golden coloured words embossed on it 'Welcome to the Pink City, Ms Natasha and

Mr Rahul.' The chauffeur guided them to their Mercedes E Class which took them to their hotel.

As soon as they checked into their hotel suite, Rahul smiled at Natasha and said, "Now would you like to stay in the hotel or would you like to join me for an experience of a lifetime."

"I would have surely told you but I guess you already know my answer," replied Natasha, barely able to control her smile.

He had his cue, and without wasting any more time at the hotel suite, they headed straight to the Mercedes that was waiting for them outside.

"You know where to take us," shouted Rahul to the chauffeur in uncontrolled excitement.

The two reached the hot air balloon site twenty minutes later, where Rahul had managed to convince the instructor beforehand that they could handle the balloon on their own and that he and Natasha did not want any third person to accompany them. Well it had taken him some convincing, but nothing that a couple of extra grand could not manage.

The air balloons' envelope had been laid out flat on the land in front of them and was covering a very huge area while the inflator fan was being placed next to the balloon to start filling it up with air. Natasha looked flabbergasted at the unfolding events. The carrying basket was then attached to the balloons' envelope and the propane burner was secured in its place. With the balloon now half full of air, the burner was fired up and the rest of the envelope got filled up in no time, rising from the ground to its full height like a magnanimous monster having woken up from its stupor. It was the most exciting sight in their lives so far, but it was just the start of the new dawn.

Once in the air, they could feel themselves floating among the clouds with no one there to pull them down. It was a magical place and they could see the entire city and the horizon which extended as far as they could see.

Ten minutes into the flight and thousands of feet above the ground, Rahul looked at Natasha, smiled, went down on his knee and like a magician pulled out a tiny red box out of nowhere. He displayed it with both hands to Natasha while opening it to reveal a simple platinum band having a small sized single diamond and the words 'NATASHA, FOREVER YOURS' inscribed on it.

"Natasha, sweetheart, would you be the grandmother of my grandkids?" proposed Rahul.

A slap on Rahul's cheeks followed, and after a few seconds of uncertain silence during which Natasha tried to look surprised but wasn't all that convincing as she had always known this would happen someday, Natasha pulled him up to his feet and kissed him like he was the last man on earth. Rahul was sure his heartbeats could be heard by the instructor in the van following them on the ground.

"Yes!" she said full of emotions in between the kissing. "I thought you were never going to ask."

Memory Wall

I'm a big fan of Bitcoin ... Regulation of money supply needs to be depoliticized.

—Al Gore, former US vice president and winner of the Nobel Peace prize

The reason Frank was very good at his work was because he never trusted emotions. He believed that emotions made people weak, and to ensure that the Noek operator's sentiments never came in the way of PAN's profits, Frank had gotten a second terminal screen of the machine's output installed in his office in Russia. He would sit in front of this screen and check on the operator's calls whenever he was not busy doing some other dirty work or cleaning up the mess that had been caused while he was setting things straight.

The only other thing apart from Frank which ensured that Noek never became an object of public knowledge was the MemoryWall. The MemoryWall was another breath-taking technology that PAN had come to acquire a few years ago. It was a blue-coloured translucent charge of dispersed electric fields which ensured that any electronic device when passed through it would get formatted. The MemoryWall had been installed across the wall containing the only door in Noek's terminal room.

Frank had got the MemoryWall installed to make sure that if any of the operator daringly succeeded to sneak into the terminal room any kind of electronic device - pen drives, mobile phones, cameras or any other device capable of storing something on memory card or hard disks - the device would get formatted as soon as the device entered into the room through the electric field created at the door by the MemoryWall.

But more than the bringing in, the MemoryWall ensured that no pictures, videos or data went out of the room, ever. It formatted every hard disk, memory card and mobile memory on any device, as soon as the device passed through it on its way out.

Besides the MemoryWall, the room's security features included the Radio Frequency signal jammer, closed circuit cameras linked directly to PAN's Russia headquarters. The RF jammers ensured that there was no kind of mobile networks available in the room, which in turn helped in implementing the statute, ensuring no operator had contact with the outside world. The only ways of contacting the outside world for an operator were the two landline phones which were tapped and all conversations recorded.

Both the phones were kept next to the terminal screen. One of them was an encrypted landline which the operator was supposed to use for calling only the shell companies present on the ledger list to inform them of their respective stock suggestions. The other landline phone had never been used by any operator till date. It came with a Russian phone number and a warning -

One Time Use. In case of emergency only.

All these security measures coupled with PAN Group's colossal pay checks to its employees and Frank's disregard for human life had ensured that no operator who ever had the slightest thoughts about breaching the sanctity of the terminal room was still alive.

Making enormous amounts of money through the predictions of a machine whose existence was a secret is one thing. But being able to keep the money safe from local authorities by transferring it over international borders without evoking interest from prying regulators and law enforcement agencies is another thing altogether.

It seemed that the PAN Group had perfected both these things.

While Frank took care of the former, it took the astuteness of Paul, the majority stockholder and CEO of PAN Group of Companies to devise a way to safely transfer the money earned in the Indian stock markets to their Russian headquarters.

Earlier, in more conventional times, Paul had devised a way in which the money in the accounts of PAN Group's shell companies was transferred manually by its employees, who every two weeks made a trip to Russia carrying the maximum permitted foreign exchange along with them.

Once in Russia, these employees would funnel the cash into the casinos owned by PAN Group, gambling and deliberately losing it away.

While the money was transferred successfully, the shell companies would put that money under various imaginary heads - Expenditure tabs of people, and setup and operational costs of machines, which had existed only on paper and nowhere in reality.

All that ever existed in reality for these shell companies was a small office, a handful of employees to execute trades and to transfer the money so earned to PAN's overseas casinos and a landline telephone.

But all this very labour intensive way of funnelling funds was a thing of the past. It all changed when the world was introduced to its most widely accepted virtual currency – the bitcoins, a virtual currency that had no boundaries.

Bitcoin is a digital currency which was presented to the world in 2009. With no central authority to monitor its usage, bitcoins had since become the de facto mode of money transfer over international borders, not only by the PAN Group, but also millions of other organisations involved in illegal activities all across the globe.

This popularity had resulted in the steady rise of bitcoin exchange rates over time, from being a meagre 0.008 dollars per bitcoin at the time of their launch in October 2009 to a massive rate of 1150 dollars per bitcoin in December 2012.

This high exchange rate had played in Paul's favour, as transferring huge amounts now needed lesser bitcoin transactions and therefore easier execution. With one bitcoin worth more than sixty thousand rupees, a transfer of six crore rupees was only a matter of a thousand bitcoins.

Things had gotten so much simpler since then that Paul had sold off the casinos he had bought earlier for the sole purpose of funnelling his money using the old school methods.

The Fine Print

When I consider life, it is all a cheat. Yet fooled with hope, people favour this deceit.

—John Dryden

The next day, back from Jaipur, Rahul spent almost the entire morning in his bed, half recuperating from the fatigue of a quick Jaipur trip and half looking forward to the upcoming Monday's meeting with Akram for final signing of the deal.

Rahul had received a call from the JONAS office informing him that the legal paperwork for their deal was ready and that he would be required to come and sign the deal papers on Monday evening. The lady calling Rahul had told him that the signing ceremony would take place at The Leela, Gurgaon instead of the JONAS offices and he was advised to not be late.

This was it. His dream, his brainchild, loads of money and fame, and most important of it all, the love of his life. While he lay in bed, he could repeatedly imagine himself saying the famous Bollywood film dialogue, only with a minor modification, *"Aaj mere paas sab kuch hai"*. His dad and brother would be so proud, but they would have to wait for the big news as Rahul had decided to keep this as a big surprise until the finalisation of the deal.

It was Sunday afternoon already, and Rahul had not even planned what he was going to wear for the big day. He jumped out of bed, made himself a cup of coffee and started planning the things that needed to be done from his side before he could go and sign the contract. He decided to go and buy himself a new suit – after all he would soon be able to afford many more suits and would be needing them for different occasions.

He picked his phone and dialled the last called number 'Nats'.

"Hey babes! Wassup? What ya up to?"

"Nothing much, was trying to find a safe place to hide the ring you gave me," answered Natasha

"Hide? Oh, I thought you would like to wear it," said Rahul, a bit disappointed.

"I will, baby, but only when I am with you. Right now I am at home, and the last thing I want to explain to mom is how you and I got unofficially engaged in a hot air balloon," said Natasha.

"That's also logical. Aunty will first have a heart attack and then throw me to the stray dogs to feast upon," said Rahul chuckling.

"No no, nothing like that. But we need to get our parents to meet sometime soon. My dad is already trying to force me to marry the son of some bureaucrat," explained Natasha.

"*What*? And when were you planning to tell me about it?" Rahul exclaimed.

"Arey chill yaar, nothing that I cannot handle. You just concentrate on closing your million dollar deal tomorrow and then we shall both go to mom and dad to put up our case," she replied.

"About tomorrow's meeting, I called you to ask you whether you can come shopping with me to MGF?" said Rahul.

"Already started with your wedding shopping, mister?" said Natasha jokingly.

And the two continued on the phone for another three hours. By the time Rahul hung up, he had already reached and explored half of the Sahara Mall.

MONDAY, 9 P.M.

The Leela was not very far from Rahul's flat. In fact, it was the last notable building before the thirty-two Delhi-Gurgaon Expressway toll gates. But just to take into account any traffic related contingency, Rahul left for the meeting almost an hour early. Rahul had never been to The Leela, and he was looking forward to this visit as one of the many firsts that were coming his way.

Rahul as usual reached well before time for the meeting and had little trouble locating the room that was reserved by JONAS Partners. Akram entered a little while later. He was alone, which was surprising, as Rahul was expecting Mukul to accompany Akram for the final deal signing. After all, Mukul was the Analyst who had apparently evaluated Rahul's business proposal.

"Hello Rahul," Akram spoke first as soon as he closed the door.

"Hey... hi, sir," Rahul fumbled in the gravity of the moment that he had been imagining continuously for the past couple of days.

"Hope I didn't make you wait too long," said Akram.

"Not at all sir, won't Mukul be joining us?" asked Rahul.

"Haha, no, he's an analyst. His work ends where my work begins, and please don't call me 'sir'. Now that we will be working together, you better get used to our company's first name culture as well," replied Akram

"Surely sir, I mean Akram," fumbled Rahul once again, his confidence seemed to have evaporated as soon as Akram had entered the room.

Akram opened the middle zip of the exquisite laptop handbag

he was carrying, sporting a black and white checkered design with a brown leather handle. He took out two sets of files and placed them on the table in front of them.

"Well, this is it then. The contracts and agreements, all in duplicate, one copy for each of us," said Akram. "You should go through them once before signing them and let me know if you still have any doubts," he continued in a very relaxed and warm tone.

"Sure, just give me a few minutes to go through it," said Rahul.

"There is no hurry at all Rahul. Once we mutually sign the agreement, then it becomes legally binding in the court of law, so please be double sure before signing anything," said Akram, hardly able to hide the sarcastic tone in his voice. He knew better than anyone that all Rahul would be interested in is the page where it talked about the amount of funding that Rahul would be receiving for his start-up.

In the meanwhile, Rahul was earnestly trying to be diligent reading the contract.

THIS AGREEMENT

('Agreement') is executed on this __ 10th ___ Day of ___ March __ Month of __ 2014 _____ Year

BY AND BETWEEN

JONAS PARTNERS INDIA PRIVATE LIMITED, a company incorporated under the provisions of the Companies Act, 1956 having its registered office at Seventh Floor, **JONAS** Towers, Connaught Place, New Delhi-110 001 and its principal place of business at Plot 121, Sector-5, Gurgaon Cyber Greens-120 301 (hereinafter referred to as 'JONAS', which term shall, unless repugnant to the context or meaning thereof, mean and include its assignees, affiliates, subsidiaries, associates, administrators and successors) of the ONE PART;

AND

___ **Rahul Kashyap** ___________, son of late Mrs Arundhati Kashyap, an individual having his registered address at __ F-22, Sector 28, Noida _____, INDIA, hereinafter referred to as '**SECOND PARTY**', which expression shall unless it be repugnant to the context or meaning hereof shall be deemed to mean and include its successors and assigns of the Second Part;

(Both '**JONAS**' and '**SECOND PARTY**' are hereinafter individually referred to as a '**Party**' and collectively as '**Parties**'.) WHEREAS:-

WHEREAS

As per the PPI directions, JONAS has obtained the authorisation from the Department of Payment and Settlement Systems, Reserve Bank of India under the Payment and Settlement Systems Act, 2007 for operating the payment system and issuing pre-paid payment instruments.

As per the PPI Directions, JONAS is required to maintain its outstanding balance {Contd. (Page 1 of 78)}

But Rahul soon realised that there was not much in these hundred odd pages of the contract that Rahul could decipher without consulting the nation's top lawyers. So he thought it wise to confirm that the funding amount had adequate number of zeroes and then sign the agreement.

"There you go," said Rahul while signing on the several pages on which it said *'SECOND PARTY Signature Here'*.

Akram picked up the files once Rahul was done and checked if any signature column was mistakenly left out. It was all perfectly done.

"Perfect!" said Akram after he had gone through the files. "Now there is just one signature which is pending from my side," Akram continued with a pleasant smile while taking out his cheque book from the other zip of his laptop handbag. He signed across an account payee cheque of ten lakh rupees - payable to Rahul.

Rahul was surprised for the second time during the meeting, "Sir, I mean Akram, I thought the cheque would be addressed to the company account that we would form for this venture and not my personal account."

"Oh yes it would. This is just a deal signing bonus for you as written in the contract that you just signed. The rest of the four crore ninety lakh rupees will go into the company account in which both JONAS and the Second Party, that is you, will be joint account holders," Akram replied to Rahul's query.

"Now go and enjoy all you can before the hard work begins in a couple of weeks. I will have my team take care of the basic infrastructure, office hunting, company formation and other formalities in the meantime. They will contact you whenever your signatures or help is needed for the same. Go now, celebrate and enjoy with your loved ones," Akram said.

Rahul was ecstatic. Ten lakhs to spend and a business of his own! He had finally done his dad and brother proud, and now he could go and talk to Natasha's dad about their wish to marry. Fuck that bureaucrat's son, Rahul thought while leaving the room.

As soon as Rahul closed the door on his way out, Akram picked up his phone and dialled the number.

"He has left," was all Akram said before disconnecting the call.

Meanwhile on the highway, Rahul's thoughts were running in all directions from his family to his friends to his love. It was celebration time for all the 'Fs' in his life, at least the first two of the three Fs.

This was the time that he had been waiting for his entire life. He was going to be rich, successful and famous. He picked up his phone and dialled a number.

Sahil Kashyap answered in a couple of rings, "What's up bro?" he said.

"Where are you guys?" Rahul asked,

"I am on my way home. Had a party to go to and now I am stuck in this stupid jam towards Noida at eleven in the night," Sahil cribbed to his brother, "while dad must be home asleep already as he hasn't called in to enquire," he added.

"Cool. I am coming home to give you both some very good news. It's been three weeks I haven't met you guys. You get home and wake up dad too. We will celebrate," said Rahul,

"But what's the good news?" Sahil asked curiously,

"I will tell you when I get home. I am driving now. Cya. Bye!" was all Rahul said as he hung up.

Rahul had just crossed the toll on the Delhi-Gurgaon expressway and the traffic was surprisingly light at this hour. "I would reach home in another half an hour," Rahul thought to himself glancing at his car's speedometer which read ninety when suddenly his car was surrounded by a couple of fast moving trucks. Soon there were four trucks; one in every direction of his car.

Rahul honked but all in vain. "These guys are not letting me pass through. Fuck man!" he cursed, when suddenly the truck that was in the front of the car noticed Rahul's dipper and started to move left.

"Finally," said Rahul to himself and pressed his foot on the accelerator and tried to overtake the truck from the right. Just then, it seemed that the truck driver changed his mind and started to move right with Rahul's car parallel to the truck. Rahul was about to hit the brakes when he saw the truck moving behind his car accelerating and coming right at him.

"What the fuck!" was all Rahul managed to say before the two trucks hit him from left and behind and moved on. Rahul lost control and the car bumped into the right divider of the highway. It started skidding left due to the impact, toppled over three times diagonally across the road before finally coming to a halt when it flipped over the highway barriers on the left and down onto the service lane.

Force Majeure

Family is not an important thing. It's everything.

—Micheal J. Fox

Natasha was preparing a Date Day surprise for Rahul when she got the news of his accident.

She rushed to the Medanta hospital where Rahul had been taken. Shiva, Arjun and Ankit were already there by the time she arrived.

"How's Rahul? What happened?" she asked them trying to wipe off the tears that were flowing down her cheeks.

"We are still not sure what happened. His car overturned while he was speeding. Some people said that he was hit by a truck but the truck and its driver are still missing," replied Shiva trying to console her.

"And Rahul? How's he?" asked Natasha sobbing.

"Sahil bhaiya has gone in with the doctors. They said he was very critical," replied Ankit, seeing Shiva not able to come out with his words.

Arjun was sitting with Mr Kashyap on the adjoining chairs, trying to take care of Mr Kashyap who was feeling too weak to even stand after hearing the news.

They saw Sahil come out of the door across the hall, eyes filled with tears.

"The doctors were unable to save Rahul," he spoke silently, hugging Mr Kashyap.

A huge gathering had emerged to pay their last respects to this ambitious young man who had never wronged anyone. The cremation ground was filled with Rahul's weeping friends and Sahil's students who had come to know of this sad news.

Natasha's parents too had come to pay their homage to this bright young boy they had heard so much about from their daughter. The parents of Shiva, Arjun and Ankit were also present, for Rahul had been like a member of their extended family.

Shiva, Arjun and Ankit were standing beside Natasha when Sahil came back after assisting his dad light the fire on the pyre. There were tears all around.

Sahil hugged the three of them. "We just lost our brother," he said out loud crying.

"I just lost my fiancée," Natasha looked down while silently speaking to herself.

For the whole of the next week, Arjun and Ankit had decided to stay at Sahil's place and help him. Mr Kashyap had not been doing well ever since he had heard the news, and someone needed to be there to attend to the grieving guests that came in as and when they heard about Rahul.

Sahil had called in and informed that he would not be joining work for some time now and that the college should arrange for a substitute teacher to take his place during this time.

Almost a week later, a couple of lawyers from JONAS Partners visited Sahil.

"Yes?" Arjun asked them as he opened the door,

"We are here to meet Mr. Kashyap in a business deal relating to Rahul," the junior of the two lawyers replied.

"I am Rahul's brother. You can talk to me about whatever this is about. Dad is not doing well and he is asleep after taking his medicines," Sahil announced to the lawyers as he joined them in the hall.

"Sure," the senior lawyer replied. "Firstly, we would like to tell you how sorry we are for your terrible loss. Your brother was a great man and his accident is a great setback for us all," the senior lawyer spouted his carefully rehearsed lines.

"Yes, yes, I know," replied Sahil as if seeing through their façade.

"We are here to present to you this cheque of rupees ten lakhs which was an ex-gratia bonus given to Rahul on signing up the deal with JONAS Partners," said the junior lawyer.

"I did not get what you mean to say," said Sahil taking a look at the cheque which was handed over to him. He showed it to Arjun who had joined them after serving the guests some water.

"The day of his accident, Rahul had signed a deal with JONAS Partners in which he had agreed on forming a new company which would work on the product, a 'Universal Card' whose patent was owned by Rahul. This new company was to receive a funding of rupees five crores by JONAS Partners, out of which an amount of rupees ten lakhs was to be transferred to Rahul's personal account as an ex-gratia amount, a 'we are grateful' bonus from JONAS. This was for Rahul's decision of transferring his patents to this new company of whom Rahul owned 66.6% and JONAS owned 33.3% shares," the senior lawyer continued.

"Now under the Force-Majeure – 'The Act of God' clause of the contract signed in between our client and your brother, in the case that something was to happen to Rahul which would have limited his ability to be full time involved in this venture, JONAS would be free of its obligation of this contract and would be entitled to choose a new CEO of their liking to ensure that the company remained a going concern and their investment did not suffer. Also in such a case, Rahul's share would be forfeited by JONAS. But in recognition of Rahul's contribution to the venture with his transfer of Intellectual Property Rights including the Patent and the B-Plan, his family would be entitled to 30% of the company's annual profits even in Rahul's absence for up to the duration of his patent expiry," the senior lawyer concluded.

Listening to what the guests had to say, Sahil picked up the cheque, and after some serious thought asked the lawyers,

"So you say this is my brothers' last earning?" asked Sahil.

"Yes sir, apart from the 30% royalty on profits that Rahul's family will receive when the product that Rahul envisioned will be launched in the market. But as I mentioned before, Rahul's death has been a huge setback to the development of this product and it can take anywhere between three to five years for JONAS to launch the same product without Rahul being at the top of this new company to handle things," replied the lawyer.

At that point Sahil returned the cheque to them.

"Please return this cheque to your boss and tell him that we are grateful that JONAS Partners had decided to help Rahul in his venture. The faith they put in Rahul's dream is more than enough for us; we don't want any money. We are happy that they are doing their best in taking forward Rahul's dream and bringing it to life. I think that is the best way we all can truly honour Rahul," said Sahil.

"We accept this cheque as well as the royalty money in Rahul's memory but want JONAS to use these funds from our side to help other kids like Rahul in realising their dreams. We would be happy if they could name the same after Rahul," Sahil added.

"As you wish, Mr Kashyap. We will surely convey your message and see to it that whether what you want can be implemented," said the lawyers before leaving with the cheque.

The Back Benchers

Computers themselves, and software yet to be developed, will revolutionize the way we learn.

—Steve Jobs, 1985

IIM AHMEDABAD, 1986

It was the decade of diversification at IIM's pioneer institute located at Ahmedabad. The silver jubilee celebrations of the institute had just ended and the current batch of students was more driven and dedicated than ever. The professors at the institute were naming it as the 'Decade of Diversification'. The Entrepreneurship Group and the International Management Group were the latest additions to this cause.

There was growth in the IT infrastructure of the institute with the campus being the first to have a campus-wide intranet access to leased lines. Internationalisation and growth were the key words of the decade, and student exchange programmes were being initiated with reputed business schools abroad.

It was a pleasant morning, and Professor Subramaniam was scribbling in his usual hardly decipherable font on the blackboard in front of a packed classroom. The topic of today's discussion was Benjamin Graham's theory of financial markets.

It was a time when serious physicists read about Sir Isaac Newton to learn his teachings about gravity and motion and serious investors read Benjamin Graham's work to learn about finance and investments.

"Known as the 'Father of value investing' and the 'Dean of Wall Street', Ben Graham (1894-1976) excelled at making money in the stock market for himself and his clients without taking big risks," the professor recited from the book. "These investments were built on Graham's diligent, almost surgical, financial evaluation of companies."

"Has anyone here heard of him before?" asked the professor to a very attentive class.

"He is best known as the guy who mentored Warren Buffett", replied one of the students.

"Yes indeed, he was Warren Buffett's mentor," replied the Professor. "Benjamin Graham in his theory states that investment is most intelligent when it is most business-like," he continued.

Professor Subramaniam continued reading from Benjamin Graham's most famous book, *The Intelligent Investor:*

"Graham notes that the 'intelligence' which the title of the book celebrates is not of the 'smart' or 'shrewd' type but relates more to the character of the investor: that is, not someone looking for a quick profit, but with a long-term view in mind to conserve their capital, who can be firm about their investing principles in the face of an emotion-driven market.

"Such a thing as intelligent speculation does exist," Graham says, "but it is dangerous when people who think they are investing are actually speculating. Any stock purchase that you do quickly, when you don't want to 'lose out on a great opportunity' is probably speculation driven by the emotions of the market.

"The intelligent investor should not get involved in trying to forecast the market's direction. This makes you a trader or speculator." Professor Subramaniam finally concluded reciting the book's text verbatim and kept down his book to write something on the board.

"But sir," interrupted a middle-aged man with long curly hair from the last bench of the left most corner of the classroom. "Where is the money and fun in that? I would rather risk it all and win nothing than keep on accumulating small change by playing it safe," he commented, his hand still raised and the artificial diamonds studded on his copper wedding ring shining brightly from his ring finger.

"What if we could design a way or train machines to automatically filter out the emotions that the market has for a particular stock and then use these market sentiments to make quick infallible profits. Wouldn't this technique be both sure shot and a quick way of making money," he continued while smiling as if he had just countered the great Benjamin Graham himself.

The attentive class suddenly became filled with commotion on this outrageous thought from this back bencher.

"But then according to Professor Eugene Fama's theory of Efficient Market Hypothesis, any technique which has the power to beat the market will be adjusted into the market as soon as the public comes to know about it, and then as more and more people start using the technique, it will no longer be effective in beating the market as ultimately it would be up against itself," blurted out a foreign student sitting on the last bench in the other corner of the room.

This foreign student was a stout little boy who was from Russia's Vlodac College and was in India as a part of one of the student exchange programmes. He had been silent and disinterested during most of the classes throughout the greater part of this semester that he was supposed to spend at the IIM, but suddenly it seemed like someone had infused a tonne of life into him. He spoke out in his baritone voice for the first time in the class since he had joined IIM as an exchange student three months ago.

The observation of this foreign student was responded by the curly-haired middle-aged man almost immediately. "Yes, exactly, and that is why we keep the existence of such a machine out of public knowledge."

Professor Subramaniam had had enough of this nonsense discussion in his classroom. His class on Benjamin Graham's logical investment theory had turned into a lesson of science fiction and he was not prepared to let it continue.

"Quiet, Mr Vijay and Mr Paul," Professor Subramaniam shouted at the top of his voice.

"Mr Paul, although I would appreciate you speaking more often in the class, but I'd rather prefer it to be on more relevant and sane topics and not some science fantasy of yours. And as for you Mr Vijay, yes sure, we can surely get such a machine to work," said Professor Subramaniam looking towards the middle-aged man with curly hair, "and you might as well ask Mr Graham to come and write the code for you," he mocked.

The entire corridor resounded with laughter, but Vijay and the stout exchange student sitting at the two corners of this classroom didn't seem to notice it. They were already lost in their thoughts of how they could make such a machine to work.

That day, on his way out of the classroom after Professor Subramaniam's lecture, Vijay was approached by the stout guy.

"Hi, I am Paul," he said in his baritone voice.

"Hi Paul. I assume we haven't met before. It was very nice of you to support me back in class," replied Vijay.

"I support things I believe in, which although incredibly rare include the thought that such a machine can be built," said Paul.

"Yes, it is definitely worth a try, but as you know, getting machines to work involves a great level of coding skills. I, with my commerce background, possess none," explained Vijay in a dejected tone.

Paul smiled at Vijay's words and explained, "Well, I won the National Coder of the Year award two years in a row in Russia," he replied.

Vijay also came to know that the Russian government had invited Paul to work for them. The perks of the job were high but the money was average and the bureaucracy bored Paul to death, so he had decided to move on.

It was as if Christmas had arrived early for Vijay, who was hardly able to control his excitement after Paul's revelation and he asked, "Would you like to move in with me? We can start working on this from today itself."

"Sure," said Paul, "but on one condition..."

"What?" Vijay asked impatiently.

"I will be the one who pays for the booze," said Paul.

"Any day," replied Vijay with a wicked smile.

Four months and hundreds of hours of exploring the theories of financial markets later, in their dorm room, Vijay and Paul were almost finished working on the machine. Vijay had indeed perfected the algorithm of value investing as proposed by Benjamin Graham and Paul had helped him in coding the same on the terminal.

Paul finally wrote the penultimate line of the machine's code. A new God of the financial world was arising.

"So what do you want to name the God?" asked Paul, looking excitedly towards Vijay.

"Ummm... I am not a big fan of Greek Mythology but I think we should name the machine *'Noek',"* said Vijay looking towards the wall clock which showed the time as 09:01 p.m.

"Is that a Greek God's name?" enquired Paul.

"Well I am not sure, but it is the Hindi translation of the time when you completed coding the God – 09:01. But it sure sounds like a Greek God. A God who has arisen to interpret the chaos of the financial markets and turn this chaos into orderly predictions."

A couple of hours later, everything was set and done. Noek had been tested internally but it still needed to be tested in real time extreme market conditions. The best fool-proof testing would have been if the God was able to take in a negative news in a positive sentiment market and still predict the upward moving stocks correctly.

The only question left was how could they make such a condition happen?

That next morning, Vijay decided to take a trip to Bombay, while Paul stayed back at their dorm room to monitor the machine's output predictions under the real time negative market conditions that Vijay had set out to create.

The machine had worked perfectly. It had taken in all the ambient real time information and come out with stupendous predictions that were right on the mark. Noek was set and raring to go.

That was a night to celebrate. Vijay was back from his short trip to Bombay and there was plenty of booze flowing in Vijay and Paul's dorm room. Four months of tremendous effort had finally paid off. But sadly, Paul wasn't drinking much on account of an upset stomach. He did not, however, let this dampen the duo's celebrations as he made sure that Vijay made up for both of their share of alcohol.

The next day, Vijay was woken up by loud bangs on his dorm room door. He was barely able to open his eyes. It was 1 p.m. already.

"How much did I drink last night?" Vijay asked himself.

"Paul can you see who it is… Paul?"

There was no reply. Apparently Paul had decided to go in for the morning lecture.

Shakily, still unable to walk straight, Vijay got up and walked towards the door.

"Coming," he shouted at the top of his voice, which was still breaking on account of the previous night's liquid adventures.

Vijay squinted as soon as he opened the door on account of the afternoon sun shining directly on him.

"Are you Mr Vijay Kashyap?" asked the inspector standing on the door in a stern voice.

"Yes," replied Vijay.

"You are under arrest," announced the inspector while he took out a pair of handcuffs and put them on Vijay's hands.

Vijay was too dumbstruck to say anything and too hung-over to think clearly as he was being taken away.

The police are in the campus and Vijay is being arrested. The news spread like wildfire across the campus.

"There must be some mistake. There has to be some mistake," Vijay kept murmuring to himself while he was being dragged away from his room to the waiting jeeps.

"No, I don't want to go. Nooo," Vijay said to the constable as he pushed Vijay into the back of the jeep.

Vijay saw Ganpat, the chai-wala amongst the crowd that had gathered to watch while he was being escorted out and shouted to him, "Call Paul, bhaiya. Inform him that I am being arrested. Tell him to come and meet me."

But Paul was nowhere to be seen.

Ⓑ

After a couple of days, Ganpat came to visit Vijay in the prison. He told Vijay that the gatekeeper and a few others had seen Paul hurriedly leave the campus premises and head towards the airport the night before the police had come in to arrest Vijay.

Vijay was not surprised.

Two days in the prison cell with no alcohol to screw his brain had made him wonder what could have gone wrong in the grand scheme of things. It was then that the realisation sunk in that Paul had betrayed him and left with their entire research to make millions, while Vijay rotted in a prison cell with no career ahead and no one to take care of his wife and two-year-old child Sahil.

Black Box

I find the lure of the unknown irresistible.

—Sylvia Earle

Today's Noek was much different from the prototype that had been tested successfully in the dorm rooms of IIM Ahmedabad almost three decades ago. With the emergence of Google and growth of the internet and social networking sites, Noek had to be adjusted to incorporate the newest sources of information that carried anything related to the public sentiments.

As these sources of information about public sentiments increased - Facebook likes and comments, YouTube channel views related to a particular news, virality of a concept, the likes and dislikes on portals, blogs, tweets and websites - information obtained by the introduction of a new source every time had to be adjusted into the machine's input variables.

It was the section that defined from which sources should the Noek pick its publically available information and then try to analyse the patterns in the chaos of sentiments. The base algorithms as designed by Vijay had remained rock solid over the decades. They had stood the test of time and hence Paul had not needed to tweak with them in any way whatsoever.

The only trouble Paul had with parting ways with Vijay and leaving him for the wolves was that till date, the functioning of the Noek had remained a black box to him, its working totally unknown apart from the input and the output. All those pages and pages of ratios and fractional values that Vijay had derived in his algorithms which were then easily converted to code by Paul. Paul, however, had no idea of how to use them in case something needed to be changed apart from the input variables.

Paul had tried several times, unsuccessfully, to replicate Vijay's model of ratios and derived differential inputs that Vijay took for the Indian markets while designing the Noek – GDP, population growth rate, GNP, FDI, benchmarked betas and several hundred other parameters – and eventually replicate Noek for other world markets, in order to make the God active in those countries as well, but to no avail. All Paul could ever match was an accuracy lesser than a monkey taking blind shots at a random stock list. Maybe he should not have let Vijay go.

But what Paul lacked in the financial aspect of the Noek, he more than made up for in the technology domain. With the advancement in technology over the years which had facilitated increased artificial intelligence capabilities in machines, Paul had managed to design and integrate a self-correcting algorithm in the Noek to make it self-aware. He coded it with the capability to monitor, analyse and compare the returns on its own transactions and transactions of other stock market players – humans as well as machines, which were performing better than its own trades – and then self-correct its code and modify its logics to deliver improved results.

The problem was, there were no human or machine which could have delivered better results than the Noek. It was the pinnacle of years of research in this domain. A fully automated system that could monitor, understand and act independently in the stock markets. The ultimate machine. A financial God.

As time had passed and Noek had proven its worth to Paul and his company, its security and anonymity had become an issue of paramount importance. Paul could not have risked revealing the code to any third person even though he had over two hundred of World's top financial analysts working for him. The question was... Could he trust any of them? Or would he commit the same mistake that Vijay had committed with him almost three decades ago?

These passing decades had not changed basic human nature, and greed and fear continued to be the two major drivers of any financial decision, no matter the size of the decision. The firm had thus far been successful in keeping the existence of such a machine a secret, maybe the best kept secret of the past decades, but Paul did not like the need to include a few more people to ensure proper maintenance and functioning of the machine.

Paul sometimes fancied believing that Noek was the only machine of its type that had existed in the world, but Paul knew the world too well to know that the chances of this being true were less than the possibility of scientists assuming earth to be the only intelligent planet in this universe.

Paul knew too well that other such Noeks, irrespective of what they had been named by their inventors, would be existing in different parts of the world, working and making money for their masters without the world's knowledge. It was only a matter of time that one of these machines would target his home turf, the Bombay Stock Exchange and then there would not be much that either he or anybody else could do about it without the knowledge of Noek's internal working and logics.

Paul often wondered about the whereabouts of Vijay, and what would he be up to? Would he have survived prison? What if he had developed himself another Noek? Could he risk it after being banned from the stock markets, and if he had managed to build himself another God, how much time would it take him to realise that his original God is still operational and the logics he developed still profitable.

After Paul had fled India on that fateful night, he had followed Vijay's trial for a couple of months during which he came to know that Vijay had been sentenced to seven years of prison and a lifetime ban on trading in any kind of stocks or commodities, whether in his or anyone else's name. A condition whose violation would have resulted in all of Vijay's financial assets being seized and frozen and he being tried again on account of multiple charges of fraud, embezzling and running market manipulation schemes. A very tough sentence by any standards, but apparently the judge presiding Vijay's case took him being a student of one of the top institutes in the country very seriously and wanted to set an example for students of generations to come.

"You are no ordinary Tom, Dick or Harry," the judge had said before delivering his sentence. "You were selected by the nation's most prestigious business school with the expectation that you would learn and do something good for the future of the country. When you decided on your own accord to adopt the ways of a scamster, you not only betrayed the trust that your institute laid in you, but you also betrayed your country," the judge had said in the final hearing of the case before passing the strictest financial industry related judgement that the nation had ever heard.

Paul had often wondered why Vijay hadn't mentioned anything about Paul or the Noek at his hearings. Was it because he was protecting his idea or was it because he had hoped that Paul had indeed not betrayed him and that Paul would watch over his family while he was in jail.

In fact, Vijay had hardly spoken at any of his court hearings. That day after being dragged away in the police jeep, Vijay had taken a vow of silence as if it was his own way of punishing himself for the terrible sin that he had committed – confiding in Paul.

But that was almost three decades ago. Over time, as Noek started earning profits for the firm, Paul lost track of his friend and colleague Vijay, who was supposedly resting in some prison in India. Paul had finally started making the money that was coming in by the kilos, just as he had always dreamed for himself.

Little did he know that Vijay was released three years early on account of good behaviour in prison and his efforts in helping upgrade the existing prison library system, as this was hardly the kind of news that made it to the newspapers; the story of a suspended IIM student's redemption. And Paul could not have cared less... but maybe he should have.

Invisible Enemy

The supreme art of war is to subdue your enemy without fighting.

—Sun Tzu

JONAS PARTNERS OFFICE, EARLY SEPTEMBER, 2014

The stock markets trading team at JONAS had by now realised they were dealing with something that was not human. Maybe their worst fears had come true and one of their competitors had come to possess the ultimate trading machine.

And what was worse than having an enemy to deal with? It was having to deal with an invisible enemy. The same was the condition of traders working at JONAS; they had no idea about who or what it was that they were dealing with.

The problem with dealing in stock markets is that at the end of the day, it's a zero sum game. You don't have to be bad to lose money; all it needs is someone who is better than you at making money. That means that your win is directly related to someone else's loss. You cannot win until the player on the other side loses; you cannot make money until someone else loses money - and no one likes losing money. Certainly not if you are losing your company's money by the millions on a daily basis on the trading floor. This was exactly what was happening more and more frequently with the traders at JONAS for some years. But every now and then, a prodigal young trader was able to pull off a blinder and make a fortune for the company, thus balancing out losses of others and keeping their division floating just above the line.

"I don't want my entire company to be filled with polished, well-mannered and customer friendly grads from the country's top B-Schools," Akram had said in one of his meetings with his HR team. "Get me kids who are hungry for success and street smart – for whom the ends matter and not the means. I want such people, people who want to achieve success as badly as you all want to breathe... and then we at JONAS will not stop as long as there is a world out there to capture."

Of late, the problem with such prodigal traders at JONAS was that they had not been able to repeat their successful trades on the trading floor for a very long time. It was as if someone was watching them trade, analysing their tricks and then using their own techniques against them in the game of stocks. Someone who was not only very fast, but very resourceful. Someone who was not only very resourceful but also very intelligent. Someone who was able to hide in plain sight and still carry out the job perfectly.

Akram had called in an emergency top level meeting in the conference room at 11.30 a.m., and although Shreya's meeting invite said nothing about the agenda of the meeting, she had an inkling that it was about the way JONAS had been losing money by the millions on the trading floor over the past few weeks. And if Shreya was right, then there would be some very tough questions coming her and her team's way, the answers to which were known to none.

She looked at her watch. It was already 10.50 a.m. and she was late for her daily catch-up with Mukul. She locked her laptop and rushed out towards the pantry. She could sense a fear of the unknown lingering in the bay as she left her cubicle and passed across other cubicles on her way to the pantry.

Mukul was already waiting for her in the pantry with her preferred decaf on a corner table right next to the television. On the screen, some of the stocks recommended by a business channels' experts along with their voluntary disclosures was being discussed.

Mukul was Shreya's MBA college friend and her love interest since their college days. They had had a history of flings that went on for a few weeks and then lost steam. When JONAS came hiring to their college, one of the top MBA colleges in their region, it was either sheer luck or a very carefully thought out move on the part of a very observant recruitment team that Shreya and Mukul were the only two who made it across all the seven interview rounds which were a part of the hiring process.

Investments can be a very tough industry, and it risks losing out great minds attributed to burnout due to inhuman work hours and work pressure. One needs to have an insatiable appetite for money and power to both enter and retire in this field - a rare combination that was immaculately personified by the person currently at the helm of JONAS.

But such a combination was very rare, and over the years, even the most promising of the new joinees had shown symptoms of burnout and had tapped out of the race after they had accumulated enough money - which did not take more than a couple of years in such a high paying industry where annual bonuses exceeded a decade's pay of an average financial sector bank job.

Thus, it was only a matter of time before Akram and his recruitment team started looking out for more innovative ways to control attrition and prevent employee burnout by giving them something to look forward to - *and there are very few motivators that supersede the chance of working alongside a potential love interest.*

As Shreya and Mukul were in charge of different teams in different verticals - Mukul's dealings primarily being with investment proposals while Shreya being responsible for trading floor – their busy schedule gave them just few minutes of catch-up time in office. The two made sure that they met for at least fifteen minutes by catching up at 10:45 every morning in the pantry for a cup of coffee.

"You are late," remarked Mukul with a wink, as soon as he saw Shreya enter the pantry.

"Well, yeah, there's a lot that has been going on in my team," replied Shreya, taking a sip of the decaf that Mukul had made for her.

"Ha-ha! C'mon, since when has that made us shorten our daily breaks," added Mukul and their conversation went on as usual.

All through her morning break, Shreya's mind was preoccupied with the upcoming meeting and its impact on the days to come.

Before long, the time had arrived and the alert on Shreya's calendar indicated that they were to make a move for the 11.30 meeting. On her way to the conference room, she saw Arvind approaching the room too. That was something out of the normal considering it was a meeting of the trading team heads while Arvind handled IT server maintenance and infrastructure for JONAS's Gurgaon office.

Once in the conference room, it did not take long for everyone to get seated across the rectangular conference table amid the paranoia and air of uncertainty, but surprisingly Akram was nowhere to be seen.

All of them waited in silence as the minutes passed by.

Leverage

When you combine ignorance and leverage, you get some pretty interesting results.

—Warren Buffet

Akram entered the meeting room after about thirty minutes. He was looking weak and it seemed as though he had not slept for days. Shreya could not help but notice that Akram was wearing the same shirt that he was wearing when she had last seen him a couple of days ago. This was unusual, considering Akram was very particular about his appearances, no matter what the situation. There was a good chance that Akram had not left office since the past two days.

"Good morning all," Akram started in a subliminal tone.

"Good morning, good afternoon," came a dispersed chorus.

"As you are all aware, we have among us Mr Arvind today, who is an expert in Information Technology, and also runs JONAS's cyber defence checks on a continuous basis. Arvind has been putting to rest any cyber threats that our company's infrastructure or our employees face," said Akram ignoring the lack of harmony in their greeting.

"Now, I had asked Mr Arvind to investigate the incidences in which our traders had lost money by the bucketful in the past few months even when all the calculations behind their position seemed to be immaculate," continued Akram.

"In fact, I was going through the very report that Mr Arvind has come up with before coming to this room," said Akram. "Without further delay, I would like to invite Mr Arvind to take stage and enlighten us all about his findings."

Akram took a seat and Arvind stood up from his. He began connecting his laptop to the projector, while everyone else in the room waited in anticipation.

"Good afternoon," Arvind started in a heavy South Indian accent, and this was the time that majority of the people present in the room realised that it was the first time they were hearing Arvind speak. Quite a few were unaware that he even existed before that day.

"I'll begin my report by coming straight to the point and not beating around the bush or sugar coating my words," said Arvind, making it very clear that he meant business.

"I have been investigating the trades made by the traders of your respective teams by examining the server calls and its simultaneous interactions made when they execute their trade calls. All I have come up in the past two months of my in-depth investigation and following these trades through millions of proxy servers throughout the world is this," he said pointing towards a blank black slide on the projector.

"Yes," Arvind continued. "A black box. I cannot tell you what exactly it is and where it is located, but what I can surely tell you is that whatever this is, it is a very cleverly written piece of code designed to manipulate the very string that stock markets run on – the Bombay Stock Exchange servers," said Akram, pausing to take in the gasping that had started among the team leaders present in the room.

"So you mean to say it is not being operated by humans?" asked one of the team leads.

"Well there is surely a human mind behind it, but the machine which is regularly beating us is not only more resourceful and much more intelligent, but is also willing to adapt with every trade that it makes."

"So is it tracking us?" asked another lead.

"Well, this machine is using the results from search engine queries - what we search for on Google and Yahoo, what is trending among the various communities, sentiment analysis from all across social media, crawlers on websites to track any changes to any of the information published on them, connotative agents, and self-learning algorithms to stay ahead of the curve - always," said Arvind.

There was a look of uncertainty on each and every face in the room except Akram's. It was as if they were being bowled an over of bouncers that were going right above their heads.

At this point, Akram stood up to assist Arvind in making the others understand what he meant with a more human touch. "In short, say if I track someone through what they post on blogs, what they share and like on Facebook, what they tweet on Twitter, what they search for on Google during different hours of the day, what videos they watch on YouTube and all their other activities across all forms of media, and then analyse which of these activities were important to them and which were done just out of an obligation to others, to predict what is happening in their lives, what are they thinking while entering a search query in Google, what is of interest to them and what is insignificant to them.

"And then predict how would all these parameters clubbed with the fundamentally available information about various stocks add up and have an impact on how that particular individual trades on a given day.

"Now imagine a machine that can track anyone and everyone who has ever traded at the stock market, and accordingly predict how the day to day events in their lives coupled with the publically available information on the stocks that they search for and in which they have shown interest will impact that stock's price and in turn the stock markets."

An uncomfortable silence engulfed the room when Akram finished. "So it basically uses all the publically known financial information about a stock, the same information that is used by our traders and then combines it with our trader's biases and sentiments towards that particular information for given stocks and predicts our trader's decisions even before they have made it on the trading floor?" asked Shreya.

"Exactly," said Arvind, "the only difference being ... it is not just us."

"And we all know that if anyone knows what trades we are going to make, then they can beat us hands down nine out of ten times. And for a machine such as this with unlimited resources and computing power, the odds rise up to ten out of ten times," added Akram.

"This means that our traders and analysts are doing all the hard work, and this machine is just tracking them through this process of their research of a stock online and then making use of their human emotions against them while using their human intelligence to trade in stocks shortlisted by them," said the team lead of the commodities team.

"Yes, so to put it in a crude way, if Shreya's team decides to buy two million shares of Tata Motors stock tomorrow, the machine will buy the stock today which will in turn lead to rise in the Tata Motors stock price by the time Shreya's team buys it and then the machine will sell the stock at the already high price to Shreya's team. Thus it makes itself a sure shot profit while our traders are left with huge quantities of an overpriced stock with no other option but to either wait for anyone else to buy at such a high price or book losses," replied Akram. "And we all know that we have been doing the latter."

At this Shreya stood up, banged a fist on the table and said, "So why us? Do we know who these bastards are?" She quickly pulled back after realising that her emotional outburst was unwarranted for in the given situation.

By this time, Arvind had disconnected his laptop, and had taken his seat among the other team leads. Akram looked at Shreya and then at Arvind and replied, "That is the point, it's not just us. The machine targets any profitable trade that it can get access to. Now, even though this greatly increases our probability of suffering from its wrath, it doesn't still explain a complete annihilation of our company's balance sheet.

"So I took the liberty of going through Arvind's report before joining you all in this room to figure out the reason for our plight," continued Akram while he connected his laptop to the projector.

And suddenly Akram bombarded his team with a flurry of questions.

"So, if I ask you all what is the one thing that we pride ourselves the most on, which enables our traders to take inhumane level of risks on the trading floor?"

There was complete silence, and everyone had their eyes on Akram as he spoke. "The one thing which multiplies our profits ten times on the one hand and puts us up for extinction on the other. The one thing that has helped us reach where we have and become who we are today in such a short span of time," he emphasised, his pitch rising while he pointed towards the screen, which had just one word on it:

LEVERAGE

Suddenly everything started to make sense to everyone in the room and a big 'Oh' could be heard through clenched teeth from several sides of the table.

"We have been long betting in markets with leverage, using money we do not own for making profits for ourselves. In fact, we have come to a stage where north of ninety percent of our trades are leveraged, sometimes as high as ten to one. So we are at the risk of suffering ten times the losses compared to if we had been betting only with the money which we had," said Akram, his pitch relatively lower and his voice much calmer.

"We are going to fall down just like the 2007 housing market in the United States," exasperated another of the TLs, referring to the colossal collapse of the US Housing Bubble, in the fall of which leveraging of bets by various companies had played a significant role.

"No, we won't. We should stop leveraging!" interrupted Shreya.

"And lose out on our huge profit margins?" said another.

"So should we knowingly risk our investors' money just for making huge bonuses for ourselves? They take the risks while we make the profits?" Shreya retorted.

The situation was fast turning into a war room when Akram finally decided to cut in.

"Enough, they very well know the risks involved," replied Akram.

"And there is no way I am letting some bitch of a machine eat up on my profits," said Akram.

"You all have been briefed of the situation which we are facing. You all know the risks and the stakes. I expect a report from each and every one of you in my mailbox with your suggested solutions to the problem at hand by five in the morning. And as none of you will be going home today, you can use your cubicles as your bedrooms. That will be all for now," said Akram, and walked out of the room accompanied by Arvind.

Garbage in, Garbage out!

The leverage and influence social media gives citizens are rapidly spreading into the business world.

—Simon Mainwaring

The next morning at 4.30, all the team leads received an email in their inboxes from Akram.

Hi All,

I hope I will be receiving your suggestions within the next few minutes. We would be meeting in the war room at 5:15 to discuss everyone's individual suggestions and then deciding upon a course of final action.

Breakfast has been ordered.

Best,

Akram

It had been almost eighteen hours since Shreya had touched her phone. She wondered how many hours more would it be before she could reply to Mukul's pings which would have been piling up.

Shreya was almost done with her analysis and running of simulations for various strategies that she could come up with in such a short span of time to deal with such an advanced and invisible enemy. But no matter whichever strategy she tested, the end results still led to a loss-making proposition for JONAS. So she had no other option but to put the same in the presentation that she was preparing to be sent across to Akram.

She was not sure what would Akram make of it given that she hadn't been able to come up with even a single profit making strategy for her team, using which they could have expected to make profits while trading in the same market as that machine.

It was 4.58 a.m. already, and Shreya was doubtful about whether the last couple of minutes could bring to her something which she hadn't already considered in the past eighteen hours. So without thinking further, she started to upload the presentation and wrote –

Hi Akram,

Please find attached my analysis of the various scenarios that we can take to beat the machine's capabilities in a fair market.

However, I would like to suggest that in the results of my analysis, it is clear that no such scenario would result in a profit making situation for JONAS except for a few outliers. Thus we would not be better than a monkey taking random bets at the market if we go ahead with any of these strategies.

Regards,

Shreya

Shreya was still considering whether or not to send the email when the clock on her screen showed **5.05 a.m.** *Meeting Reminder – Meeting in ten minutes*

She clicked on the SEND button on the top right corner of the screen and left for the meeting room.

In the conference room, Akram was wearing the same white shirt with fine royal blue pinstripes for the fourth consecutive day, the only saving grace being that everyone else was in same clothes as the previous day as well. A true trademark of a hard working office, or a copyright of an office in distress.

The TLs were still joining in as Akram and the others who had already arrived settled down and prepared to discuss the points covered in their respective presentations. That morning, unlike the day before, Akram had arrived before time, just like a commander waiting to be given the good news of his army's spoils by his generals. But the grim faces of his generals said otherwise.

"Shall we begin?" asked Akram, looking across all the team leads who had joined in. "Yes," came a suppressed chorus reply.

"Speak up guys, boost up your energy levels," spoke Akram in a raised voice after hearing such a dull response.

"Haven't you guys had your morning tea?" Akram asked rhetorically and without waiting for any replies dialled the pantry's number from the intercom lying next to him.

"Nine black coffees in the conference room please, and send them fast," ordered Akram to the pantry boy who picked the intercom.

"This shall wake you guys up, now let us begin," said Akram with a wave of his hands as if he was declaring the opening of the national games.

"Let's start with hearing the lady first", said Akram pointing towards Shreya who was the only lady in the room.

"Well, I, …ahh, yes," mumbled Shreya totally caught off-guard.

Akram in the meanwhile had put up Shreya's presentation on the projector screen which she had mailed to him a few minutes earlier.

"Well," she began, gaining control of her confidence and her words. "I would like to share my suggestions with the team..." she had just started speaking when she was interrupted by Akram.

"Skip the customaries Shreya. Lets come directly to the point. We have a machine to kill," said Akram trying to pump in some enthusiasm in his team,

"Yeah sure," she replied now totally back from her trance. "So, as you can see, I shortlisted several non-conventional strategies for trading in a fairly regulated market. I then ran extensive scenario tests on each of these strategies and came up with aggregate results."

Shreya paused as Arvind walked into the room. He was looking all fresh and lively with a new set of clothes. Apparently he was the only one who had the opportunity to go home and sleep tight. She continued after a brief pause, "But as is evident from the charts so obtained from the scenario analysis of the shortlisted strategies, we do not end up in a profit making situation in any scenario if we exclude the outlier values."

"So what do you propose from this analysis?" asked Akram who was also carefully going through the presentation for the first time.

"Well Akram, I would suggest that..." she paused in between her sentence as if revaluating the outcome of what she was about to say on both, her individual career path and on the company's profits.

"Well, I suggest that we suspend any trading in the stock market until we can figure out a comprehensive strategy that shows positive results in all scenarios," she concluded.

The room was suddenly filled with murmurs which were silenced as soon as Arvind, the newest entrant in the room, started speaking. "This comprehensive strategy of yours would have a self-defeating purpose," he said. "As soon as you use your new profit making strategy, the machine will notice what you did to beat it, will learn from it and then implement it even before you can use the strategy for a second time. Why else do you think all your existing strategies that you took from a manual failed in your scenario analysis?" asked Arvind.

"Well then sir, I have no further suggestions that could be of any use to the room," replied Shreya, her disappointment clearly evident in her voice.

"That is it? That is all you could come up with in one complete day assigned to you particularly for this task?" spoke Akram in a tone of such sarcasm that Shreya felt like an ostrich in search of a place to hide her face.

"This is a real disappointment and waste of time guys, please if any more of you have wasted your and the company's time on such useless analyses, please speak up now to avoid wasting everyone's time any further," shouted Akram looking across the room.

"These are desperate times, and they require desperate measures," Akram continued. "Now me your desperation. Your desperation to succeed, your desperation to win at all costs, and your desperation for your next seven-figure bonus," he shouted even louder as if the commander was prepping his generals to go for an all-out attack on their enemy.

"Do not expect me to care for rules, because I don't expect you to pay any heed to any rules either. We are at war, and all I want from you is victory. These is no such thing as fair markets; there are either profitable trades or unlimited losses. And losses would not get you your next bonuses," continued Akram in his elevated pitch. "So if anyone of you has a suggestion different from Ms Shreya's suggestion, speak up now, or we will go back to the drawing board all over again and meet again at ten tonight with your new suggestions," his speech was paused by the arrival of black coffee, which was no longer needed as every soul in the room was wide awake and high on adrenaline as if they had just jumped out of a moving plane.

Only two people raised their hands which was more than what Akram had expected.

"Yes Gaurav, what do you have to suggest?" said Akram, regaining his calm and a composed tone.

"Akram, why don't we go public with the news of the existence of such a machine, and give it an evil name for fetching it visibility among the non-concerned audience, say *Money Spy,* claiming that it is a machine that eats away your money as soon as you invest in the stock markets," suggested Gaurav.

Akram was happily surprised to hear Gaurav come up with such an idea. The idea seemed good, but Akram had his concerns.

"We cannot prove its existence to anyone until we agree to have deployed unethical counter measures ourselves to track and discover such a machine's existence," said Akram.

"And moreover, it won't stop only at our admitting to having deployed such measures. To prove the machine's existence, we would have to open up our offices and server logs to the investigative agencies in support of our claims, and although I doubt they would find anything objectionable that we haven't already hidden or erased, but that might be a risk that we should not take willingly. It would be like inviting the wolves into a sheep farm," added Arvind, concerned about the long term effects of such a strategy.

"Yes, I agree with Arvind's opinion on this. We can at no cost let the government agents crawl over our private matters," said Akram, now realising the full scale impact of following what Gaurav was suggesting.

"Sir, pardon me for saying so, but considering we are in a *no-rules-apply* kind of a situation," said Gaurav, laying full emphasis on the words 'no rules apply', "shouldn't we buy this proof of the machine's existence that we need from someone in a position to sell it. I am sure Mr Arvind would be able to track down the right person for us, and as we know, there is always someone ready to sell whatever you need, at the right price," he added.

Akram looked at Arvind as if enquiring whether what Gaurav suggested could be done.

"Well given some more time, I can hack into the stock exchange servers and track down the IP addresses from which the buy and sell orders received at the exchange originated, but we cannot be sure whether the machine is at that location too or is it being operated from somewhere else," replied Arvind in response to Akram's glare.

"In any case, it is a risk worth taking then," replied Akram, finally having hope that his generals might not be all that useless after all. "Arvind, you'll be tracking down the address and location from where such requests are coming and Gaurav, you'll approach and negotiate the price for buying the proof of the machine's existence – hard copies of trades, photographs, log files, anything and everything that is on offer, and as you said, no matter the price," said Akram with a scheming smile.

Shreya could not have felt more out of place after looking at Akram's face as he uttered those final words – 'no matter the price'. She felt she would puke, but she knew even that would be a waste of effort in this case.

"But Akram, tracking them down will not happen immediately; it might take us some time – days or even weeks. Considering the last time you asked me to find out what was going wrong, it took my team of hackers almost three weeks to track the existence of such a technology. The machine is using state of the art techniques to avoid being tracked. We might have to track it through thousands of proxy servers spread across the globe to reach its real location," said Arvind, trying to bring Akram's expectations in pace with the timelines they were looking at.

"Can't we get it done quicker?" asked Akram having no idea about what Arvind had just said.

"Unfortunately Akram, we won't be. Our machines have their limitations when it comes to getting into proxy server logs using brute force attacks," replied Arvind, this time himself not sure about how much of what he just said would Akram actually understand.

It was all German to Akram, and all he could say was, "Okay, but try completing it as soon as possible."

As soon as the topic was over, Akram turned to his only remaining general who offered a ray of hope.

"Yes Gautam," pointed Akram towards the lean fair guy with wavy hair sitting next to Shreya on the conference table. "You had something to say?" Akram said referring to him raising his hand earlier.

Gautam was the team lead of the metals division and was famous in JONAS as Mr Flirt. There was no girl Gautam would not date given a chance, and those who had been on a date with Gautam would agree that it was worth every second of their time.

Gautam started in his sonorous voice, "Akram, during my days at IIT, we used to study a concept that was referred to as 'Garbage In-Garbage Out. Now what it basically meant was no matter how well-written a program's code is, the program and the code in itself are worthless if they are not given the right inputs. Say for example, we have an immaculately written program whose purpose is to add any two positive numbers. Now no matter how huge or how small positive numbers you pass as inputs to the program, it would always give you the right result."

"But," he continued, "the problem for the program starts occurring when you start passing it negative numbers or imaginary numbers; numbers which the program's code has not been written to handle. We called such an input as garbage for the program, as no matter how small or how easy the addition for these out of scope numbers may be, the computer program will process them only as it has been coded to, and in turn deliver wrong and faulty results as the output, thus in turn making the output nothing more than garbage itself," explained Gautam.

There was a look of accomplishment on Akram's face, as if he was for the first time seeing a younger version of himself. While on the other side of the room, Arvind was cursing himself silently for how on earth he could have missed what Gautam was about to suggest. It was so simple a strategy that the thought of such a strategy being effective in a situation as complex as theirs had completely evaded Arvind.

"So what I suggest is," continued Gautam, already aware from the look on Akram's face that whatever he was going to say had already been approved, "that as Arvind was suggesting yesterday, the machine derives its input information from all across the internet looking at what people share and search on internet and then comes out with a prediction of what possibly is the best output given the inputs it has picked. So, if we were to somehow add a lot of nonsense data and contradicting statements about public sentiments in that input stream, thereby greatly affecting the quality of the machine's input, the machine would be none the wiser to differentiate between what we can refer to be authentic input data and what we can call noise or nonsense input data," said Gautam.

He continued, "And therefore the machine would suffer greatly in its ability of picking quality stocks and beating other traders. All it would be giving out would be names of garbage stocks based on the junk and misleading information it takes in as the input for its predictions, fundamentally misleading information that would be spread virally across the internet using our virtually unlimited resources," Gautam concluded, his chest puffed out and his heart thumping as if he had just finished delivering his acceptance speech for the Economics Nobel Prize.

"Brilliant," shouted Akram at the top of his voice. "Arvind, clutter the information that the machine takes in and the general public gives out, and make the information as deceptive and counter intuitive as it can get," he said looking towards Arvind. "Now tell me at least this is possible without any major hiccups?"

"We can use bots. It has been done before but never in the financial industry," said Arvind and continued after a long pause of digging out some files on his laptop.

"There was this article in the *New York Times* sometime back which says and I quote," said Arvind, "During the 2012 presidential elections in Mexico, the Institutional Revolutionary Party, or PRI, was accused of using tens of thousands of bots to drown out opposing parties' messages on Twitter and Facebook. The PRI is said to have employed a little trickery, parsing and twisting language enough to confuse people about what the opposition really meant to say online. In Turkey, where Twitter was briefly banned not long ago, an investigation found that every political party was controlling bots that were trying to force topics to become trends on social sites that favoured one political ideal over another. The bots would also use a political group's slogan as a hashtag, with the intent of fooling people into believing it was more popular than it really was."

"Awesome then, I love these politicians. Get on it right away. We will be the first ones to use this technology in the financial markets," Akram ordered Arvind.

"Garbage in, garbage out! Fantastic!!" repeated Akram to himself.

"But Akram, should we not do a complete analysis that such a step..." Arvind was in the middle of completing his suggestion when he was abruptly interrupted by an excited Akram.

"And let the machine rip off our investors' money in the meantime?" said Akram. "You have my orders, please get back to Gaurav as soon as you are able to locate the IP address for him. In the meantime, get our resources to flood the internet and social media with misinformation until we have completely demolished this machine's prediction capability."

"And how would we know that the machine has been destroyed?" asked Arvind in a rebellious tone.

"We would know when our traders start printing money again. Until then, don't stop," were Akram's final words before he concluded the meeting and finally went home for a change of clothes.

Reminiscences

If you don't like how things are, change it. You are not a tree.

—Jim Rohn

THURSDAY, 1 JANUARY 2015, 7 A.M.

The new year had finally brought some great news for the JONAS Partners.

Within three months of the fateful early morning meeting, traders at JONAS had booked more profits than in the last year together. Gautam's strategy was working and the machine was losing its hold on the stock markets. What remained to be seen was how long it would be before the machine adapted itself or was reconfigured by its owners to cope up with this new threat.

In the meanwhile, Shreya had constantly been contemplating after that day's animated early morning meeting about whether or not she wanted to work at JONAS any longer, where she got no respect. After these many years of working at JONAS, money had not remained a vital motivator for her anymore.

It had been almost three months since the thought of quitting JONAS first made home in Shreya's conscious. She was thinking of telling this to Mukul whenever she met him next, considering that these extended work hours in the past few months had ensured that even their bare minimum fifteen minute breaks were ssible and that they were unable to see each other ys at a stretch now, thus eliminating the second and only other motivation apart from money for Shreya to keep working at JONAS.

As the entire country celebrated the New Year's Day with zeal and enthusiasm, Mukul had decided to take Shreya out for a date on this one day company holiday to discuss something important with Shreya, as he had mysteriously told her.

He had booked them a room at a private property that went by the name of Golden Turtle Farms. It was a privately-owned, professionally-managed farm house cum recreational weekend getaway about thirty kilometres from Gurgaon on the Manesar border. Mukul had suggested that they leave at night so that they could have some private time together in their room as the clock turned twelve. Shreya, however, had insisted for a morning drive instead, just to avoid being stranded on the roads when the calendar turned, given the terrible traffic in Gurgaon due to the New Year festivities.

Mukul picked up Shreya from her South Ex house at around ten in the morning. The traffic was light and the GPS on Mukul's phone showed an ETA of one hour and fifty-two minutes later.

"What could the number mean? And who is Sahil?" Paul asked Frank looking at Noek's latest prediction.

"I would have said that it maybe his Social Security Number, but in a country like India things are never so simple, apart from the fact that they don't have social security," spoke Frank in his thick Russian accent.

"Hmmm, you are right, things are never simple with the Indians," spoke Paul as if in deep thought.

Paul had been awake in his study for the past eight hours since the New Year had started and the God machine had encountered its first anomaly in the span of twenty-eight years.

He had been going through bundles and bundles of files containing some kind of ancient code and algorithms. A code that he had not looked at for more than a decade now. He was trying to figure out the probable cause of this unlikely behaviour of the machine, and this ancient code and its corresponding documentation which was written at the time of Noek's development might somewhere contain a clue to the same.

All Paul hoped to find was a single name, a single line that could somehow connect to his search of who Sahil Kashyap was, and why Noek had given out his name.

The name had a familiar sounding ring to it. All Paul had to figure out was what.

The weather was in Mukul and Shreya's favour as they reached Golden Turtle Farms. It was a much more secluded area than Mukul had originally imagined and what the website had described. But as soon as the couple entered the gates of the farmhouse, they were pleasantly surprised by the serenity and ambience of the place.

The property had a mini golf course adjacent to the entrance followed by a swimming pool and its adjoining benches. As they parked their car, they could see the beautiful lush green gardens with exquisite sofas laid out for the purpose of soaking in the radiant sunshine on this winter morning of a new year.

"So, Mister," began Shreya continuing with their on-the-way conversation. "Finally we have arrived. So what was it that you wanted me to wait till here before telling me?" asked Shreya settling down on one of the two sofas right next to the swimming pool boundary.

"What do you think it is, Mistress?" asked Mukul while picking up a cup of hot chocolate that the waiter had brought in as their welcome drink.

"Umm, how would I be knowing now," she smiled expecting Mukul to ask her out for marrying him.

"Well take a wild guess," said Mukul.

"Well, Mister... I would say that you want to ask me to marry you," said Shreya deciding to cut the chase and end the foreplay as she wanted to tell Mukul about her decision to quit JONAS before she said yes.

Mukul suffered a mild shock. The conversation that he had in mind had nothing to do with marriage. On the contrary it had to do with separation.

"Shreya, I don't want to offend you. I am flattered, but if I may say the truth, I am taken aback a bit by what you just said," replied Mukul.

"So you were not going to propose to me?" asked Shreya candidly, thinking that was an even better opportunity to tell Mukul about her decision to quit.

"I would truly love to propose to you," Mukul said, "if you are ready to marry a soon-to-be unemployed guy," disclosed Mukul without any hesitation.

"What?" shouted Shreya loud enough for the waiter standing at the pool's other boundary to turn and look at them.

"Yes," replied Mukul. "In fact, this what I was talking about when I mentioned on the phone that I wanted to discuss something important. I wanted to talk about it here, far away from office, before I made my final decision and put in my papers."

This time, it was Shreya's turn to be shocked.

"But why Mukul? Has something happened?" asked Shreya out of concern, deciding it may after all not be the right time to tell Mukul about her decision to quit JONAS as well.

"Yes," answered Mukul in a very grave tone. "I have reasons to believe that I may be an accessory to the murder of a young innocent boy," his voice almost broke up as he coughed up those words.

"And I cannot just live with it and continue working here," he added.

"What?" said Shreya so loudly that this time the waiter actually approached their table to enquire whether everything was ok.

"Yes," said Mukul to both the waiter and Shreya, listening to which the waiter reproached to his original place.

"I think that I may have assisted Akram in the murder of Rahul, a young entrepreneur whom I was following up with last year around this very time."

"But how Mukul? And Akram committing murder? He is a complete asshole but I don't think he could be a murderer, and trust me when I say I have zero regard for that guy," said Shreya.

"Even I did not think so. I have always known Akram to be a guy with zero respect for rules and laws, a guy who only cares about the ends, no matter the means. But even then I did not think he could stoop so low just to protect his investment," Mukul paused in between as if having second thoughts about whether he should disclose any more to Shreya.

"What is it Mukul? What is bothering you so much? C'mon tell me," Shreya insisted, sensing his hesitancy in disclosing any further details.

"I don't think you should know any more than this. I have already told you enough. I don't want to put you in any kind of danger," Mukul spoke in a concerned voice.

"Oh c'mon, you know me much better than that. You know what, I will make you a deal," said Shreya. "You be frank and open up with me on this and I will be frank and open up with you about what I have decided."

"You have decided? About what?" asked Mukul out of curiosity,

"I will tell you when you tell me. Quid Pro Quo," replied Shreya.

"Okay fine," said Mukul. "You don't have to play games with me. I was just concerned about your safety."

"And I am about yours, so tell me," argued Shreya.

"A couple of days ago, while updating some new year investment deals related articles in the archives of our news database, I came across this online article that mentioned a terrible accident involving a budding entrepreneur that had taken place on the Delhi-Gurgaon highway around February last year," Mukul started. "It was not until I had read through the entire article that I realised that the person the article was talking about was the same whom I was assisting for investment by JONAS's Investment Division."

"So what does a random and unfortunate road accident involving an entrepreneur have to do with Akram being a murderer?" enquired an inquisitive Shreya.

"Concerned about missing this news around that time and out of curiosity for that boy and the deal which I had suggested to Akram in my presentation, I researched a little further just to discover that the deal which Akram and that boy allegedly signed never made it to JONAS's financial filings for the last fiscal year," continued Mukul.

"So what's the big deal? Taking into account the terrible loss of life, Akram might have decided that it would not be ethical to print money on a dead boy's idea, and might not have included the deal in the financial filings altogether, especially as probably no or very little exchange of funds took place," replied Shreya, although considering the thought of Akram not making money on account of some ethical dilemma was nearly impossible.

"Even if you believe that Akram would be considerate enough to let go of such a thing," said Mukul with a bit of sarcasm after sensing the uncertainty in Shreya's voice while she made an attempt to provide a possible explanation to what might have actually happened he continued, "How would you justify Akram restricting me from following up the deal and ensuring that he was the only one who was in touch with the boy from JONAS's side from the point I gave him my report to the date the boy died. Their last meeting was completely off record and off the company expense sheet," he continued.

"What do you mean exactly?" asked Shreya

"The day Rahul died in that freak road accident while going back from Gurgaon to Delhi, I remember Akram mentioning to me that he would be meeting Rahul at The Leela around the same time on that day. He also insisted that he would like meeting the boy alone in a private room meeting after I told him that I should be the one assisting him as per protocol.

"And what's more, I visited our projects folder yesterday on the main server, and guess what, no records of any scanned soft copies of any agreement being signed between JONAS and Rahul, and no record of the ownership of the B-plan that this boy had. It was as if that meeting never took place. No paper trail at all, except my, and am sure, Akram's reminiscences," concluded Mukul.

Shreya by this time had realised that Mukul's fears were not baseless and what he was saying made a lot of sense.

"Should we go to the police?" asked Shreya.

"I thought of it too," said Mukul, "but as I just mentioned, there is no proof to substantiate what I am saying. It would be my word against Akram's, and with JONAS's money backing him, he would bury me deep under defamation lawsuits which I would spend my entire life fighting," replied Mukul, his agitation with himself clearly showing on his face.

"But we cannot just stay quiet and not do anything about it, and let that motherfucker destroy lives of other such innocent people," replied Shreya, clearly agitated.

"That is why I have decided to quit. If I could not stop it from happening, I sure am not going to be a part of it anymore," replied Mukul making his point crystal clear to Shreya.

"But Mukul, there must be something to indict him," Shreya was literally begging Mukul at this point.

"There is nothing, Shreya. He is too smart to leave any proof. Just the unusual and mysterious circumstances under which Akram had asked me to not follow-up with Rahul after his meeting, and the absence of any records of the same, followed by Rahul's death, and the story of his missing patent. I have gone over all of it, I have gone over all of it," replied Mukul almost talking to himself. "The point here is, can we really do something?"

"We will think of something, I promise we will," Shreya said holding Mukul's hand.

"So what is it that you wanted to tell me?" asked Mukul trying to divert a discussion that was not taking them anywhere.

"Ohh that! Well I have decided that I will be quitting JONAS," said Shreya with a wink.

Fear of Greed

Greed is not an issue of finance. It's an issue of the heart.

—Andy Stanley

"Tell me you have some good news," shouted Paul as soon as he saw Frank enter his office.

"Have I ever brought you any bad news?" replied Frank smugly.

"Nopes, apart from the past few weeks when you have brought me no news at all," taunted Paul. "There is no news on the curious case of Sahil Kashyap" said Paul mockingly.

"Well, If that's what to want to hear," said Frank with an air of attitude. "I have located your boy wonder," he added.

"Wow! Now that is good news! Now I would have asked you how but I know better than to ask you about your dirty ways and your elaborate network of informers," Paul smiled. "So tell me, what were you able to find?"

"For now, just the address and occupation," Frank replied. "But I will have much more soon."

"Hmm," Paul murmured waiting to hear the details.

"He is an assistant professor of finance at the IFT Institute in the Qutub Institutional Area of Delhi, lives in a 2 BHK rented flat in Noida with his father," said Frank. "Nothing exciting. No boy genius or a wonder hacker as you might have presumed. Just a random normal guy making his day to day living," replied Frank.

Paul smiled. "Well he stopped being normal the moment the world's smartest machine gave out his name with a buy recommendation." "Any information on the number?"

"Still working on finding the significance of the number."

"Work faster and get back to me as soon as you find anything. And in the meantime, book me a ticket to New Delhi. It's time to meet the God's buy prediction face to face," said Paul.

"Sahil sir, there is someone to meet you at the reception," the peon informed Sahil in the staff room.

Sahil wondered who had come all the way to the college instead of his house to meet him. He entered the reception to find a stout man who did not look like he had come from any place nearby.

"You must be Sahil," said Paul in his baritone voice.

"Yes, but I am sorry, do I know you?" asked Sahil, a bit puzzled.

"No, I am afraid not. But that is why I am here. To introduce myself to you and to know more about you," replied Paul. "Can we go to someplace more secluded?"

"Yes sure," said Sahil surprised at the visitor.

"We can go to one of the empty rooms. Please come," said Sahil, leading Paul to one of the lecture halls that was empty.

"So what can I do for you Mister..." Sahil hesitated realising that he had not even asked the name of the stranger.

"Paul," replied Paul.

"Mister Paul," repeated Sahil.

"Well Sahil, I would get directly to the point. I have come all the way from Russia to recruit you," said Paul

"You what?" asked Sahil with a smirk as if he had not heard Paul correctly.

"Yes, you heard me correctly. I want to hire you to work for my company, the PAN Group of Companies."

"Oh, so you are the Paul of the Paul And Nathan Group of Companies?" asked Sahil in disbelief.

"Indeed I am," replied Paul.

"What would the owner of such a big multinational want with an assistant professor like me?" asked Sahil curiously.

"Well, I would want to offer you a job," Paul replied. "A location near your place in Noida and fifty times your current salary," he added.

"Fifty what?" Sahil almost shouted in surprise. "I am sorry, sir, but I think you have confused me with someone else. I think you should leave now."

"What's wrong?" enquired Paul.

"Well, just that I don't believe anything that is too good to be true, because usually it isn't. Plus, I love my current job and the relation I have with my students is something money can't buy. I don't want your money. It is not what motivates me. I am not one to take decisions based on greed. I have seen far too many people get destroyed because of it," replied Sahil.

Paul was taken aback a bit. Who says that kind of shit, he thought to himself. If money does not motivate you, you need to go to an asylum, he thought of telling Sahil but he thought maybe he should offer Sahil something even better.

"What about an opportunity to study and operate the world's most advanced financial machine? A financial God in its own doing," Paul proposed

"I am sorry, Mr Paul but your riddles are beyond my comprehension," Sahil replied.

"Allow me to explain myself." Paul smiled. "Let's say, and I am just assuming a completely hypothetical situation. Let us say that there existed a machine that could predict the stock markets, a machine that can observe traders, learn from them and then adapt itself to predict what trades they would make even before they have made those trades, a machine that could analyse such information across the entire market and finally come out with which stocks are going to be profitable," Paul paused for a brief moment.

He looked at Sahil and continued, "Let us say such a machine existed, a machine code-named Noek. As a person who has dedicated his life to the study of finance and financial markets, wouldn't you like to be near it, Mr Sahil? Would you not want to flirt with the God's mind?" Paul concluded his sales pitch, realising that Frank would have to eliminate Sahil in case Sahil did not agree to join, considering the sensitive information Sahil was now in possession of.

Sahil was flabbergasted. There were no words that could describe his state of mind. On the one hand he was tempted to say "fuck off" to Paul on account of his disregard for Sahil's earlier decision and his continued persistence; on the other he had known the world a little too well to not realise the death threat that came with not accepting such an offer.

"I need some time to think," was all that Sahil said.

"Sure Mr Sahil, take all the time you need in the world. But just to be clear, such exclusive offers are a 'limited time only' offers," Paul winked seeing Sahil's wry smile at his words.

"I know Paul," Sahil said politely pointing Paul out of the room.

Paul started moving towards the door and the suddenly turned back.

"And now that you already know so much about us, would you please help us by letting us know whether this number means anything to you?" said Paul taking out a piece of paper from his jacket containing the number which the machine had given along with Sahil's name.

Sahil had a long hard look at the number.

"No sir, it is the first time I have seen this number," replied Sahil, looking into Paul's eyes while talking to hide his lie.

"Fair enough," said Paul. "Keep the chit in case you come across the same number anytime in future," Paul said on his way out.

Numbers Game

A good decision is based on knowledge and not numbers.
—Plato

Sahil had a fair idea what the number that Paul showed him was about. Although he did not remember it completely, the type of numbers were a part of ICICI banks, in which Sahil had once opened his trading account a long time ago.

He came back home and searched for his documentation of his account to find his exact account number and the account's password which Sahil had long forgotten.

Sahil finally found the account opening documents. He pulled out his account number and the numbers were an exact match to the number on the chit that Paul had given him.

What could Paul possibly be doing with an account number to a bank account that Sahil had not used in ages, he wondered. In fact, Sahil was sure that the bank account would have turned dormant by now because of its non-usage.

Just for the fun of it, Sahil tried his luck by signing into the account, certain of the fact that it would result in a 'Dormant Account Sign In Error'.

The browser was taking its time to open the page but it wasn't the error page that it had opened. Sahil was able to sign in and was redirected to the bank's security message page:

Sign in Successful. You last logged in on 16 January 2015, 2:14 p.m.

"January 16? Today? How could that be possible?" Sahil said to himself and went straight to the Account Summary page.

To his astonishment, the summary read-

Assets - Rs. 70, 89, 32, 674.53

Liabilities - Rs. 0.0

Sahil now knew what his dad was up to during the entire day when Sahil was at work.

"Dad!" Sahil shouted at the top of his voice from his room.

"Yes," came a mild reply.

"You better be able to explain this," he scolded.

Mr Kashyap entered the room to see his trading account open on Sahil's laptop. The cat was out of the bag and Mr Kashyap had a lot of explaining to do,

"From where do I start?" he asked without trying to act smart.

"From the very beginning, Dad, from the very start," replied Sahil.

"During my days at the IIM," Mr Kashyap started revealing, "I, along with another guy named Paul came up with this idea of making a machine that could take in ambient information and predict the markets on its own. This idea consumed us like anything and we started working on it continuously day and night for four straight months before we finally built it."

Sahil was listening in pin drop silence, surprised to hear Paul's name, the guy who had become a big threat for Sahil out of thin air in just a couple of hours. And there Paul was again, resurfacing through his dad's past.

"I was the brain and Paul was the hands," his dad continued. "I wrote the logics and he coded it. But to be sure that our machine worked, we had to test it for real-time extreme market conditions, and what could be more extreme than a bomb scare at the Dalal

Street itself. We decided that one of us would have to take the risk of going to Bombay and spreading a hoax threat of a bomb being placed on the Dalal Street. I decided to take the risk as Paul had to stay back and observe the machine's output. I went to Bombay from our Ahmedabad campus and successfully unleashed panic among the traders trading on the street during those days. The market reacted to the sentiments of fear and uncertainty and the Exchange Index declined on this widespread bomb scare news. But our machine had worked. It had predicted the stock prices of various stocks that would end up rising even in a declining market," his dad said, a smile on his face as if he was reliving the time and the success of that day.

"Paul had confirmed that the machine was errorless, and I returned to our campus that very night. Paul got me profusely drunk that night giving the excuse of our celebrations, and he took off with all the code and the logics that we both had worked upon for months. The next day the police traced me to our campus and I was arrested. I refused to say anything in my defence and so the judge sentenced me to jail. What was worse was that I was banned from trading in the stock markets ever again," continued Mr Kashyap in a dejected tone.

"So I started trading using the strategies that I had perfected, using your account which had gone dormant. I got it reactivated in your name and have been spending time building my family a small fortune to leave behind when I am dead. Rahul and you would not have had to live the life of misery that you both had been living with me alive," said Mr Kashyap, saddened by the realisation of the fact that this dream of his was to be left unfulfilled forever after Rahul's death the previous year.

Sahil was left flabbergasted for the second time in a single day.

"But why didn't you say all this in court?" asked Sahil.

"And laid to waste the biggest invention of this century?" counter questioned Mr Kashyap. "I was young then and maybe stupid. Maybe I should have said all that in court then, but I didn't," he added.

Sahil had a living example of what could happen if you let your sentiments and morals rule you in front of Paul. He could not afford to repeat the same mistake that his father had made Mr. Kashyap had already lost one son; he would not be able bear the loss of a second within a span of one year.

If Sahil did not act prudently, this might very well be the end to his bloodline with no one remaining to continue the Kashyap surname.

And the first step that he had to take in this direction was to decide whether or not to tell his dad about Paul being able to locate them after all these years. And whether to share his newly-acquired knowledge of the current day's Noek which was stolen away from his dad decades ago.

Sahil decided that his dad had already lost enough in his life on account of Paul; he could not let Paul do the same to him or his dad again.

"Dad," said Sahil, "there are some things that I think you should know."

Frank had, in the meantime, returned to India to assist Paul with Sahil's background search, armed with his newly acquired knowledge of the same.

He met Paul at two in the morning in Blue Bar at Hotel Taj where Paul was staying.

"I have the information that you wanted on our wonder boy," said Frank sipping his scotch.

"Hmm," came Paul's usual reply, urging Frank to continue.

"The number that we were so desperately trying to figure out... Sahil's ICICI bank account number," continued Frank, "which as of today reads a total balance of more than seven hundred million rupees."

"That's an impressive amount for a teacher who is not motivated by money," Paul pondered aloud.

"Yes, and it is a demat account," added Frank.

"Even more strange considering Sahil's views about money. Anything else?" Paul asked indicating he was about to leave and go to his room.

"No, nothing much apart from this. Father's name is Vijay Kashyap, brother's name Rahul Kashyap..." Frank was reading from his phone when Paul interrupted him.

"Did you say Vijay Kashyap?" Paul repeated, suddenly sinking deeper into his sofa as if he had nowhere to go now. "That's why the name sounded so familiar. It was not the name, but the surname."

Market Research

If we knew what it was we were doing, it would not be called research, would it?

—Albert Einstein

Shreya and Mukul had been searching about Rahul extensively on the internet. They were surprised at how much the internet had to offer about someone as common as Rahul. With some simple queries on Google, they were able to get his address from voter's list, his father and brother's names as well as his other family details.

They came across Rahul's Facebook obituary account, a service by Facebook that converts the FB profile of any person who is dead into his memorial page. People had commented their thoughts about Rahul on his obituary page, and Mukul noticed one person's reply to all the 'Rest in Peace' messages on the page. Sahil Kashyap had ensured that his brother's page was not left unanswered.

"I think we should meet Sahil and tell him about his brother's death," said Mukul to Shreya while staring at his MacBook's screen.

"But what would we tell him?" asked Shreya.

"The truth, what else?" Mukul replied.

"But as you said, we have no proof," she debated.

"We don't have proof to get Akram convicted in the court of law. We don't need proof to tell Sahil that his brother's death was not an accident but a murder," he replied.

Shreya knew Mukul had a point. Sahil had the right to know the truth about his brother's death. She gave a nod to Mukul indicating that they should go ahead with the plan.

Mukul opened Sahil's profile from Rahul's page and clicked on the 'Message' button.

Hi Sahil,

I am Mukul and I somehow knew your brother. I want to talk to you about his death. Please do not talk to anyone else about this. You might put my life in danger. Let me know if we can meet and discuss.

Mukul decided not to mention the details about his encounter with Rahul at JONAS to avoid raising eyebrows in case Sahil decided to talk to anyone else at JONAS before coming to meet him.

Shreya had decided to come along with Mukul to his meeting with Sahil. She was not sure what to expect and she was not even confident that they were doing the right thing.

"Once we do this, we are done with anything connected to Rahul's death," Shreya said to Mukul on their way to the meeting point. "You can have a clear conscience that you did all that you could by taking the risk of telling the truth to Rahul's brother," she added.

"I will try to. At least I will be able to sleep properly at night," replied Mukul.

"Yes, and then we will get married and I will not let you sleep," Shreya winked.

They reached Building 5 of DLF Cyber City where they were supposed to meet Sahil at the Chayos Chai Café, an open tea bar.

Both of them ordered a Pani kum Chai as they waited for Sahil to enter through the glass doors.

Sahil entered a few minutes later and shook hands with Mukul. He was not sure whether Shreya knew who he was or was she just Mukul's accomplice.

"You said it was something related to Rahul's death?" Sahil started.

"Yes," replied Mukul looking across to Shreya, anticipating her to take the conversation forward. There was a moment of odd silence between the three.

"We wanted to tell you that Rahul's death was not an accident but a well-planned cold blooded murder," Shreya finally spoke after a deep breath.

A Random Walk

Coincidence is God's way of remaining anonymous.

—Albert Einstein

"Are you sure you want to do this?" asked Mukul, seriously doubting that Sahil would be able to hold himself together if he came face to face with Akram

"Am I sure?" Sahil replied with a counter question. "You come and tell me that my brother was killed because this man... your boss could not have enough fun with the money he already had, so he found killing an innocent boy who trusted him as a profitable investment. Even then you are not sure how many such Rahuls have fallen prey to this boss of yours! And then you ask me whether I am sure that I want to meet him? Of course I want to meet him, and then I want to destroy him," said Sahil, his voice shaking heavy with anger.

"This is the very reason I am sceptical that you should meet Akram. You would not be able to resist the urge to hurt him and might end up doing something stupid. Akram is a smart guy. It will not take long for him to find out who you really are and then hurt you and also put all of us in danger," Mukul said with a great deal of concern.

It suddenly dawned on Sahil that everyone who was running a financial company wanted to eliminate the Kashyap clan from the face of the earth.

Shreya had been silent for most part of this meeting before she spoke up, "Even if we assume that you would not end up doing something stupid," said Shreya realising from Sahil's expressions that he was not going to stop anyway, "even then, why would Akram want to meet you? He is the head of one of India's most well-known financial companies. He does not meet any random guy just because one of his employees want him to do so."

"Then find him a reason why he should be interested in meeting with any random guy. He is your boss; there must be something that you know - perversions, addictions, money. Anything. All I need is one meeting with him where I can look him in the eye, gauge him and ask him - how much money is finally enough?"

Shreya and Mukul looked at each other.

Mukul finally spoke, "Sahil, he has his sources sorted for all his perversions and addictions, and he has not gotten to the level he is today by trusting random people with his best kept dirty secrets."

"So you are telling me that there is nothing Akram wants that could make him risk meeting a guy he does not know?" asked Sahil, a bit surprised as well as agitated.

"Well there is this one thing," Shreya spoke suddenly and then quickly lowered her voice, as if realising what she was about to suggest might be a bad idea.

"What thing?" asked Sahil.

"No nothing. You would know nothing of it. Some strange and weird stuff," she replied.

"Try me," said Sahil. "After the kind of people I have met over the past few days, I doubt there is anything left in this world that can be categorized as strange."

"Well... in the past few months, he has had this infatuation about a machine that JONAS's competitors have possession of, and Akram wants to buy proof of its existence. He has tried everything in his power to destroy the machine and it seems Akram is currently successful in distorting the machine's ability to trade. Still Akram is not satisfied because of his inability to completely kill this enemy," Shreya stopped midway after noticing the sudden change of expressions on Sahil's face which was raging with anger now.

"Sorry, I didn't intend to say that. All I meant was that he does not believe in just letting is competitors walk away," she said, quickly apologising for her uncanny reference to Rahul' murder.

"What kind of machine?" asked Sahil, not responding to Shreya's apology.

"Well, it is some kind of artificial intelligence that learns, adapts and trades on its own. The machine's heroics have caused significant losses in the past to JONAS as we have been leveraging a lot, and this machine learns how our traders think while trading on the basis of their search queries and online presence. And once it learns how they think, it then beats them by predicting their next move beforehand," replied Shreya with little hope that Sahil would have understood at least some of what she said.

Sahil on the other hand was surprised to hear this approximately same description of a machine for the second time in as many days. It could not be a coincidence, Sahil thought to himself. This had to be the same machine which Paul had approached Sahil for. The same one that he had offered Sahil to work on.

But for this to be the same machine, there were two things that were essential.

Firstly, Sahil had to be a very lucky man, as he would be the only dot connecting warring financial giants which were hell bent on hurting each other, two financial giants whose leaders had in the past taken away something which was very dear to Sahil. One had taken away his father's hard work and freedom, while the other had taken away his brother.

And now Sahil was at a crossroad where it all came together, where he possessed the information which both these parties would kill for, again.

Was the Noek correct about its final prediction? Was Sahil to be the next outperforming stock which both these companies should have bought into their team?

But sadly, both these companies had already sold off Sahil and his family, and in stock markets, unlike in life, there are no second chances.

And secondly, for the two machines to be the same, Shreya and Akram's interpretation and description of the machine had to be wrong. After all, the machine did not trade on its own.

"What are you calling it? This machine?" Sahil asked Shreya.

"That's the funny thing, we don't even know what to call it, and Akram claims that he has already disabled it," replied Shreya.

"Fix me a meeting with your boss. Tell him I have all the information that he needs. I am no longer any random guy. I am the most important person he would like to meet in his life," emphasised Sahil.

"What? And then what will you do when you meet him? You won't have anything to offer and then he will get mad at me. Not that it matters to me anymore, now that I have already decided to quit," questioned Shreya candidly.

"You came here seeking redemption for what your boss did to my brother, and to absolve yourself for your part involvement in Rahul's death, right? Do this and you can go home with a clear conscience. Be sure of the fact that you have given Rahul's brother a standing chance to avenge Rahul's death," said Sahil in an appealing tone, looking at Mukul who had been sitting quietly for the past fifteen minutes.

Hearing this, Mukul looked at Shreya and then back at Sahil.

"We both wanted Akram punished for the wrong he did to this boy, didn't we?" Mukul finally broke his silence and spoke up to Shreya.

"Yes," she replied.

"Fine, then let's do this and finish it once and for all," Mukul said imagining Sahil would do the worst when he actually met Akram. Little did he know that Sahil had other plans.

"And for you, Mr Sahil, this is the last time we meet. After we do this, we are even," said Mukul in a firm tone as if it was some kind of negotiation and Mukul had just given Sahil his final offer.

"Likewise," replied Sahil.

"Fine then," added Shreya. "I will call Akram from the car itself on our way back."

The three got up and shook hands for one last time. This was farewell to Sahil and Rahul as far as Shreya and Mukul were concerned.

"And oh yes, one last thing that I have to tell you," spoke Sahil while on their way out, his finger pointing towards Shreya, "They call this machine 'The Noek'."

Shreya was left standing with an amused smile on her face.

"Yes, Shreya," said Akram blankly picking up his phone, not feeling the need of adding any customaries.

"Evening Akram. I wanted to let you know that I have located the guy that you wanted Gaurav and Arvind to find," said Shreya.

"What? You can't be serious," replied Akram in a truly surprised tone. "How did you do that? Frankly speaking, Shreya you were the last person in that meeting room that I would have expected to come out with something useful," said Akram.

"Yes, I realise that I haven't been at the top of my game lately," she replied, sarcasm flowing through her words, but Akram had his attention fixated on the content of the words rather than the tone. "Consider this my final comeback."

"How did you manage to find him?" asked Akram again

"I wouldn't bother with the specifics if I were you," she replied, all the while thinking what an interesting reply it would be if she had included the specifics. He is the brother of the guy you killed last winter, she thought to herself.

"I have touched base with him and he is willing to sell the information we need given the price is right," Shreya added.

"How much is he demanding?" questioned Akram.

"He won't say until he meets you personally," replied Shreya playing her masterstroke.

"Hmm ... if this is what it takes. Set up a meeting with this guy of yours," replied Akram.

"Sure, will do," she said, "and yaa...they call it The Noek," added Shreya before disconnecting the call.

"Congratulations. I have just handed you your prey. Happy hunting. Roast it well and have a feast," Shreya messaged Sahil as soon as she disconnected Akram's call. "The Great India Place Mall, Noida, Food Court, coming Wednesday at 5 p.m. Don't be late," she added happily.

"I never am," came Sahil's reply.

Window Dressing

If you can't make it good, at least make it look good.

—Bill Gates

Consequent to the details that Frank had illuminated Paul with, Paul was of the opinion that it might be the case that Noek had improvised based on the artificial intelligence and self-learning algorithms that Paul encoded into the machine in the past several years. When Noek was itself unable to make genuine profitable trade predictions due to some external forces manipulating with its input data, the machine would have kept scanning for better profit making benchmarks and eventually come up with a bank account that was constantly better performing than the machine itself. A bank account number with a buy call on the name of its owner would have been the God's way of telling Paul that there was someone better which it could not match any longer.

As Frank had informed Paul that Vijay was still banned from the stock markets, Paul knew he would surely have been trading under Sahil's account. A fact that the machine could have never known. All it could recognize was the use of the algorithms that had formed a part of the machine's very core.

Paul would need to meet Sahil again and this time ask him to take his offer even more seriously, if not for his sake, then for the sake of Paul's oldest friend and the machine's father. The machine was in need of its father again, and Paul held the key to this father through his only remaining son, Sahil.

"If the machine as you mentioned it to me actually works, why haven't we seen PAN Group's profits skyrocket to the moon?" asked Sahil as soon as he saw Paul at the Taj's Café Coffee Day.

Paul had invited Sahil to the Taj CCD for their second meeting. It was one of the few outlets open till the wee hours of night and was just across the street from the hotel where Paul had stayed put since his arrival in India. It had been a long time and Sahil had not gotten back with his decision on whether he would be joining PAN's operations. Paul needed to decide on whether Frank would have to dispose two more bodies or not.

"Would you like to have tea or coffee?" Paul answered Sahil's question with his.

"Nothing. Just answers," replied Sahil,

"You will have all the answers you seek once you give us your decision," Paul insisted.

"What difference does it make, before or after? If I don't join you, I am dead anyway," announced Sahil in a matter of fact tone.

"Yes, I find fear to be a very effective motivator," replied Paul. "It always seems to work, even at places where money doesn't."

"Yes, I agree with you on that. Fear is a very effective motivator. It makes you commit such terrible crimes which even money can't," replied Sahil, thinking about what Akram had done to Rahul.

"So how is it that you have kept your stock prices from exploding even with your ever increasing profits?" Sahil went back to his original question.

Paul was beginning to like Sahil's attitude. There was something different in him today, something that Sahil had lacked in their first meeting. A kind of killer instinct. A go for the kill attitude.

"Firstly, Mr Sahil I would like to correct you. The machine we had *was working*. It is currently, well let's just say, facing some issues with its prediction capabilities," Paul started. "And secondly, Mr Sahil, I assume you being a professor of finance would be well-versed with window dressing techniques used by private funds to overstate their profits."

"Yes I am," replied Sahil.

"Well, then let's just say we Reverse Window Dress," replied Paul trying to be as vague as possible.

"You'll have to give me more than just riddles to help me help you Paul," said Sahil.

"Help you help us?" Paul asked taken by surprise.

"Yes! I know all about what you did to my dad and the origin of Noek," he replied pausing in between to let Paul take in what he was saying. "I also know that the reason you were so desperate to hire me was because you needed my dad's help in fixing something that must have gone wrong with your machine that even with all your resources, you have not been able to fix."

It was Paul's turn to be left startled.

"But I cannot help you until you help me understand how this entire system of yours works. I need to know the story in its entirety. Only then I'll be able to ask my dad about what could possibly be wrong," Sahil continued.

"Well excuse me, Mr Sahil when I say that I don't trust you and your sudden change of heart," Paul seemed sceptical.

"Well, you don't have to trust me. As I said I am not in it for the money. I have plenty of money, so I won't betray you for that." Sahil was confident, thanks to the fortune in his bank account. "I am in it for the very same reason that my dad has kept the existence of Noek a secret even after you betrayed him. For the knowledge of the pleasure and possibility that the existence of such a God offers. It is an academician's ultimate prize, the Mecca of knowledge," he added, getting slightly emotional.

Paul was beginning to get convinced that Sahil meant no harm and that his sudden change of heart might be what was needed to awake Noek from its stupor.

"Fine Mr Sahil, I believe you. But please remember, as much as I dislike using fear as a motivator, I will make your worst fears come true if you ever try to take advantage of this mutual trust of ours," Paul said in a threatening tone.

"Well, as I said, I won't be your normal guy for operating Noek. I will just be a consultant with resources that have expertise in the field of your need," said Sahil referring to his father as a resource. "So I won't be taking any money from you and will not be trading through your God. The aim is purely academic and the purpose purely professional."

"Very well then, you will know whatever you want to know. Come take a walk with me," Paul said, getting up from his chair.

Back from the CCD, Sahil - now armed with his newly found knowledge of Noek directly from Paul's mouth - was lost deep in his thoughts. He was trying to work out and plan his next move, when he suddenly picked up his phone and dialled Natasha's number.

"Hello," said Natasha.

"Hey Natasha, I need you to do something for Rahul."

In the meantime, back at the Blue Bar after the meeting, Frank tried to warn Paul of Sahil's intentions.

"I like this boy of Vijay's," said Paul, a little too drunk for the night. "He reminds me of myself when I was young. Let's just hope he does not try to repeat what I did to Vijay when I was young. I would hate to kill him."

"Okay, if you say so. I will let him play around the Noek, but will kill him at the first sight of any harm he intends to do," Frank replied.

"The machine gave out his name. Let him have a go at it. And the machine is already in sleep mode. What more harm can this boy possibly do?" said Paul sliding down his sofa with another glass of scotch while Frank watched on.

The Dilemma of Morality

Commerce without Morality. (one of the seven deadly sins.)
—Mahatma Gandhi

Akram came to meet Sahil at the Great India Place food court. Akram began, "My people tell me that you won't discuss the price of the information we seek with anyone else but me."

"Well, I like dealing directly with the person who is capable of paying me. Middle men are such a pain in the ass," replied Sahil.

Akram was already impressed with his counterpart's attitude.

"Sure, true that. In a country like ours, paying money for getting things done is not the problem. It is finding the right person whom you can pay money to get things done which is the bigger problem," said Akram.

"Sahil," Sahil introduced himself.

"Akram, but I guess you already knew that," said Akram extending his right hand for a handshake while introducing himself.

There Sahil was, shaking hands with his brother's murderer. While he was shaking hands with Akram with his right hand, the fist of his left was clinched so tightly that his nails dug an inch deep into his skin. If only Sahil had a gun to shoot Akram right then, but a quick death would hardly have been the revenge Sahil was seeking. Sahil had things worse than death planned for Akram.

"So what information can you give me about this magical machine that scans, analyses and operates like an unstoppable wild elephant in this financial jungle of ours, treating us like we are some kind of expendables?" said Akram getting straight to the point without wasting any time.

"Well, do you really think the machine has been empowered to act on its own? Would you give a machine the ultimate freedom to act God…to buy and sell stocks using your company's money? You surely are not naïve enough to believe it yourself now, are you Mr Akram? Because if you are, then I'll be putting myself at great risk by dealing with you. We should probably end our meeting here itself. Fools are such a liability," Sahil told Akram as he looked on in disbelief.

Sahil was still able to manage a façade of a smile on his face, though his arms and wrists were as tight as a boxer's in a boxing match, waiting to deliver his knockout punch.

"I would tread very carefully with my words if I were you, Mr Sahil," Akram responded immediately. Sahil had managed to hurt Akram's well-guarded self-esteem. No one talked to Akram in such a manner.

"But you are not me, Mr Akram," said Sahil in an attempt to agitate Akram even more, wanting Akram to lose his cool and show his real self.

"Just tell me your damn price and you shall have it. I want proof that you possess knowledge of the machine's existence. Let us spare the theatrics. That will not get you anything," said Akram, suddenly changing his tone and growing impatient of having to deal with a nobody.

"You may pay the damn price and you may have the damn information, it hardly matters to me. But the question is – will you be able to bear the opportunity lost by what you are planning to do with that information? Can a man like you be so ignorant about the possibilities that he has. Could your knowledge be so limited?" said Sahil talking in riddles and further infuriating Akram.

"Oh, in case you have forgotten, it was I who stopped this machine's rampage. What is it that you can possibly know that I don't already know? The very reason that I am sitting here talking to you is because I am in need of proof that can be held in front of SEBI to ensure that this beast of a machine never raises its ugly head again," Akram finally said cutting down the power play of the cat and mouse chase that was resulting in him being humiliated by this nobody.

Sahil had achieved what he wanted and had been able to put the exact question in Akram's mouth which he had been so long waiting to answer.

"Well, I for one know that Noek does not automatically pull off trades by itself. That all it does is suggest an eligible stock and its probable trade to the operator in charge of it, and it is up to the operator whether he wants to act upon it or not. And I know for a fact that the machine is still fully operational and working flawlessly." Sahil delivered his master stroke.

"And how would you be in possession of such information?" asked Akram, still surprised by Sahil's revelations.

"Because..." said Sahil after a deliberate pause, "I am the machine's operator."

The knockout punch had been delivered successfully to the opponent. Sahil was no longer a nobody for Akram.

"Why are you telling me this? Why not just give me the proof I need of the machine's existence, take your money and disappear?" was Akram's next, rather obvious question.

Sahil had Akram dancing to his tune now.

"Because I am in some way like you, Mr Akram," said Sahil.

"I don't get you," said Akram.

"Money," replied Sahil.

"So you want me to give you money in return for this information as well?" Akram asked with a sly smile on his face. His confidence returned with the belief that he had finally seen through his counterpart – just another common man trying to bite off more than he can possibly chew.

"No," replied Sahil.

"Then?"

"On the contrary, I want both of us to make money," said Sahil.

Akram seemed a bit confused. "What do you mean to say exactly?"

The second of Sahil's questions came out verbatim from Akram's mouth. It was quickly becoming a one-sided match.

"Well, when I give you the proof of the machine's existence and you anonymously spread it across all media using your contacts, the news and the buzz in the media about the machine would definitely raise the regulators' eyebrows and would lead to a SEBI enquiry," said Sahil thoughtfully.

"Well, that's precisely the plan," said Akram.

"Well, then the Noek is going down for sure, and once it goes down, a miracle of a machine, a God in its own saying will be lost forever. But before that happens, as it would conspire, you and I stand in a position to make lots and lots of money using God's work," said Sahil.

He had Akram's full attention so he continued his well-rehearsed selling pitch, "Till now, I have been passing on Noek's stock suggestions that it delivered to me at a remote location in Noida to the PAN Group's analysts situated in Mumbai so that they can invest PAN Group's money in those stocks. But what if in the upcoming few days, I were to pass Noek's suggestions to JONAS first and then wait for you to fill up your accounts with the stock and then pass on the same stale information to the PAN Group?" suggested Sahil, improvising and playing on the details of Noek's working which he was now in possession of, courtesy his last meeting with Paul at Taj CCD.

Akram seemed elated. The possibility of the God that had caused them so many losses working for JONAS was too good to be true. It would be a dream come true for Akram. But how could Sahil be trusted?

"So you mean to say you would be betraying PAN right in their office?" said Akram trying to test Sahil's intentions.

"Money knows no sides. And morality is a dilemma I least expect a man like you to be worried about, Mr Akram," Sahil replied, hitting the final nail in the coffin.

Akram didn't seem to mind the sarcasm this time around; he had grown used to it.

"Hmm, you may be right about me, but I am more interested in your demand," said Akram trying to regain control of the conversation that had long been controlled by Sahil.

"Fifty percent of the profits made," said Sahil confidently without a bit of hesitation.

"What? Fifty percent? Are you out of your mind? It is me who is taking the entire risk, remember?" shouted Akram.

"And it is me who is providing the entire reward," replied Sahil in the same pitch. "Risks and rewards go hand in hand, Mr Akram. You don't need me to remind you, do you now?"

Akram was taken aback by Sahil's response. Sahil certainly wasn't in a mood to negotiate. He meant business and so did Akram. The only question that remained was could Akram trust him.

Akram was caught midway in an investor's dilemma. It was greed versus fear – greed of being able to use the God's infinite wisdom of financial markets versus the fear of being betrayed by the person who was offering the key as the priest of this God's temple.

Would he make the same mistake as most of the investors make? Would he let greed get the better of him?

"Alright," said Akram. "We have a deal. I'll invest the money and you bring me the information. But the information better be correct, or I will find you and I will hurt you bad. Please remember that, Mr Sahil, if you ever think of betraying me," concluded Akram, unable to stop his greed from getting the better of him.

"Don't worry, Mr Akram. If you lose money, I lose my profits, and I don't like working for a lost cause. This is the beginning of a very profitable relationship for both of us," replied Sahil.

"And just as a token of our good faith," continued Sahil adding fuel to the fire, "a little birdie tells me that the PAN Group analysts had strict instructions to not miss out on any trades that were known stronghold investments of JONAS, something to do with maintaining your dominance by hurting your enemy badly, they said," added Sahil, ensuring that this instigation was motivation enough for Akram to do what Sahil planned him to do.

Akram was left red-faced when Sahil left the room, still infuriated about Sahil's last revelation. So his team's concerns about JONAS being targeted by their competitors were proving to be true. No one turns on heat at Akram without getting burned themselves. Sahil had just handed Akram a flamethrower.

As soon as Sahil left the hotel room, it was his turn to make a call.

"Yes?" said the girl on the other side of the phone.

"The fish has taken its bait. The plan is on," said Sahil and hung up.

The moment Sahil disconnected the call, Natasha knew she would have a lot of convincing to do the coming Sunday morning to get Mr Sethi help them with Sahil's plan.

Deal or No Deal?

I no doubt deserved my enemies, but I don't believe I deserved my friends.

—Walt Whitman

"Dad, I need you to do something for me," said Natasha that Sunday morning.

"What is it, baccha?" Mr Sethi responded, looking at his watch while taking a sip of his green tea and wondering how come his daughter was wide awake on a Sunday morning instead of afternoon. Little did he know that she, Sahil and Rahul's friends had not slept a wink for the past two days because of their extensive planning, the entire execution of which hinged on Mr Sethi's approval of what Natasha was going to ask of him.

"First tell me that you will not say no," said Natasha.

"Well, that depends on what you ask for."

"Dad, I am serious. It is for Rahul."

Natasha's dad put down his cup of tea and faced his daughter, "What are you up to Natasha? I told you that it was an accident. You have to get over it and move on."

"Dad, those people killed Rahul in broad daylight. How can you tell me to move on? These assholes need to be brought to justice," said Natasha, not realising her voice had risen enough to reach her mom who was reading the *Sunday Times* in the adjoining room.

"What happened, beta?" her mom said walking in.

"Nothing Mom, you continue your work. Dad and I were having a general discussion," said Natasha trying to persuade her to go away.

"She's still not over Rahul and still believes in the conspiracy theory that his death was a murder and not an accident," added Mr Sethi laying waste Natasha's attempt to not involve her mom in their discussion.

"What?" Mrs Sethi exclaimed. "I thought we were over with this discussion long ago. I don't want you to suffer like this over something that you cannot change. Now please forget it and let us plan something nice for the day."

Mrs Sethi looked at her husband before going back into her room. "Dilip, now that Nat is up early, let us go out for a nice lunch at the Oberoi's."

"You heard mom, better get ready fast," said Mr Sethi to Natasha.

"Dad!" shouted Natasha intentionally. "I haven't slept the past two days and I am going nowhere until you talk to me and agree to what I am asking."

"You haven't what? Okay fine, tell me what you want from me?" complied Mr Sethi.

Natasha finally had the Director General of Telecom's undivided attention. All she had to do now was to make it count.

"Dad, I would have tried to show you proof of how Rahul was murdered at Akram's order. He is the MD of the financial giant JONAS Partners, but I know you don't subscribe to conspiracy theories and Akram is too smart to leave a trail of evidence. I doubt dwelling on why I am doing what I want to do would be of any use in front of you," she started presenting her case with the lines that she had rehearsed over and over in her mind at least a hundred times the previous night.

"I will come directly to the point," she continued, "I need your help in doing something that is, well not exactly legal. Sahil bhaiya and Rahul's friends have devised a way to get justice for Rahul, but we will require some experts in the field of technology to help us out."

By this time, Mr Sethi had completely forgotten that there was an unfinished cup of tea lying in front of him. He had even started forming the opinion that his daughter getting up late on Sunday afternoons was not such a bad thing after all.

"All we need for Sahil bhaiya's plan to work is that we delay the feeds of stock prices that reach JONAS offices by a couple of minutes. We have to make sure that the delay is across all media of communication – television, internet and even phones."

Natasha continued, "And we need it to be effective for at least a couple of hours so that in the meantime. Sahil bhaiya is able to convince Akram and his team that Sahil bhaiya actually has control over the Noek. Then, we can have them dancing to our tune," Natasha finally concluded.

Mr Sethi suddenly felt that that he had entered his midlife crisis all over again. He simply did not know what to do about his daughter who was on the verge of turning into a vigilante and in the process, making him break half a dozen laws. Moreover, he did not understand half of the things that her daughter had just said, and what was a Noek? thought Mr sethi to himself. It would have been so much easier if she could have asked him for a new iPad instead.

"Natasha," Mr Sethi had just started speaking when he was interrupted by another outburst from his daughter.

"C'mon Dad, you have always taught me to stand for what is right no matter what others think, and for something to be right, it does not have to be proved right to you first. I know what I am doing is the correct thing to do, and if you don't feel it's right, that does not make it wrong. I have made up my mind and now it is up to you to make your decision. Will you or will you not help your only daughter?" said Natasha with a puppy face in order to bring in the emotional aspect to the bargain.

Mr Sethi had seen a lot during his long and successful career. If there was one thing that he had learned better than anyone else was to realise whether he had been cornered or not by the opposing party, and then to get himself out of such a situation. The realisation that his only daughter was trying to strong hand him had sunk in for Mr Sethi and it was time for him to do what he was best at...talk tough business.

"Enough," said Mr Sethi in a stern tone. "You do not get to lecture me on what is right or wrong. Do you even realise how many laws I will be breaking if I agree to do what you are asking for? And that in no way means that I can do what you are asking of me to do. I am not even sure I can contain such a conspiracy if I ask someone in my department to get such a thing done."

Natasha was taken aback a bit, and a short pause followed.

"And the risks are many – my job, our family's security, prestige in the society – everything that your mom and I have worked for our entire lives. Plus, child, these are very powerful people that you are deciding to choose as your enemies. And people who do not choose their enemies wisely end up not going very far in their life's journey," Mr Sethi concluded.

"Well Dad, I have made my decision. It is time for you to make yours," said Natasha quietly but in a reluctant tone.

"I will obviously not let you go on a suicide mission without making sure that you will get out of it alive. I will do whatever needs to be done, but I need a promise from you as well."

"Anything Dad, anything," said Natasha, a smile lighting up her face.

Mr Sethi waited a couple of seconds before his next words to add a sense of importance to thc words. It was a technique he had long used in his business circles before making important announcements, to ensure that his words were never taken lightly.

"After all this is done and dusted, you will marry the guy your mom and I choose for you and when we tell you to. No more 'you have not gotten over Rahul yet' and other of your excuses of you waiting for the Mr Right. Pay your last tributes to Rahul with whatever you have planned to get him justice with and then move on with your life with a partner of our choice. This is the deal; take it or leave it!"

It was as if Natasha hadn't heard a word. She was quiet, so her father added the final word, "Now you can think over it while you get ready for the lunch that your mom has proposed for today afternoon. In the meantime, I will discuss the same with your mom."

As soon as her dad had laid down the terms of his allegiance in front of her, Natasha realised how her dad was so successful in his professional career. This man knew what to say and when, and how to manipulate people into giving him what he wanted. And now that she had seen her dad pull that off against herself without any prior notice, she knew she could depend on him to deliver what she was asking if Natasha agreed to his terms of the deal.

Natasha was about to trade marrying a man she would never love against justice for the man she always loved but could never marry.

"It's a deal dad, it's a deal," she said softly to herself looking at Mr Sethi go and talk to her mother in the other room.

Red Herring

Our wisdom comes from our experience, and our experience comes from foolishness.

—Sacha Guitry

A couple of days later while she was driving, Natasha got a call from a blocked number on her cell.

"Am I talking to Miss Natasha?" a voice which was young and cold asked from the other side of the phone.

"Yes, speaking."

"I am the man who has been put in charge of taking care of the deal," the voice replied.

"Ohh, so you had a talk with Dad, he told you everything..." Natasha was speaking when she was interrupted midway.

"We will not take any more names, and no specifics. This is a private line but I have been explicitly ordered to not leave any trace. I have been briefed on your disposition and I will take care of the technical end of the things," replied the voice from the other end.

"Wow, that's great," said Natasha, with a smile that would have made even the cold voice on the other side of the phone warm if he had been in front of her.

"I will need the date and time during which you plan to carry out your operation along with a few other details," the voice continued.

"You will have it soon."

"And I cannot guarantee against complications from any external sources not being altered and monitored by my team. The risk and responsibility of this lie completely on you and your team," concluded the voice.

"Yes, I understand. You will have my and my friends' full support," replied Natasha.

"I will call after two days. Keep the date and time ready," came the response, "and it's not us who needs support," he said before he hung up.

"Wait, but how will I contact if I need to?" Natasha tried enquiring but it was too late. The phone had already been disconnected.

As soon as Natasha reached home, she dialled Sahil's number.

"Sahil bhiaya, Dad delivered on his promise. I just got a call from some blocked number asking me for a date and time for the plan," Natasha spoke while parking her car.

"That is good news."

"Yes, but we are not ready yet. He told me he will call back in two days for a final confirmation," said Natasha.

"We all need to meet and finalise our strategy tonight itself then," Sahil suggested.

"Yes, but where and how?" asked Natasha.

"Can we meet at your rooftop like we did the last time?"

"We can, but I'll need to sneak you guys up. I don't want us to be seen by dad. It might get real awkward," said Natasha, not wanting any of them to meet her dad to avoid any discussion of the terms on which Mr Sethi had agreed to help them.

"Okay, if you say so," replied Sahil, unsure as to why would it get awkward as her dad was willingly helping them.

"Cool then, I will get in touch with the others. You be there at our point at nine sharp. I will meet you there," said Natasha, referring to the Samosa Junction that was just two minutes away from her home. It was where all of them including Rahul used to occasionally hang out.

"And I will lure in our target," said Sahil referring to Akram.

Sahil dialled Akram's private number from his cell. He picked up the call after seven rings.

"It took you quite long to answer the phone. I thought you were no longer interested," Sahil began trying to establish his supremacy over the ensuing conversation.

"Come to the point, Mr Sahil. We would not be having this conversation if both you and I were not greatly interested in minting some money, and moreover I had to get my employees out of my room before I could talk to you. I cannot be having this conversation in front of them," was Akram's stark reply.

"Sure you can't," replied Sahil with a sly smile.. "Anyway, I have good news. I have arranged for a special burner phone to be delivered to you in a couple of days. It can't be traced back to me even if someone gets their hands on it. All future communications that we would have would be on that number."

"Well I must say I don't get your gimmicks, Mr Sahil." replied Akram.

"These won't seem as gimmicks when some competitor or SEBI will investigate to link JONAS's increasing profits with its access to inside information, no matter the source of this insider information. Better safe than sorry, Mr Akram. You should not leave a trail of bread crumbs," replied Sahil.

"Fine, I will be waiting for your parcel. Call me when you have a stock name," said Akram desperate to end this conversation that was not making him any money.

"I will, and I never said it was a parcel. Have a good day, Mr Akram," one of your last good days, thought Sahil. The fish had been lured to take the bait.

That night Sahil was joined by Shiva, Arjun and Ankit at Samosa Junction. Natasha arrived in her car shortly after. As the junction was more like a roadside stall with a couple of benches on the adjoining footpath, the guys saw Natasha's car as soon as it came within sight. They got into her car without delay and Natasha started to take a U-turn towards her home.

"You should do some walking, you lazy bum," Shiva mocked Natasha.

"Uff, shush. The car will get you all in directly through the garage door without anyone noticing you," replied Natasha.

"What? You are already treating us like escaped convicts," said Arjun.

"No baba, just a precaution to avoid any of us being seen by dad. He has agreed but I don't want him to get all worked up about us and then go back on his word," said Natasha, not realising that Sahil had noticed the hesitation in her voice about her dad for the second time during the same day.

They all reached Natasha's house, and she asked them to tip toe to the roof while she got water bottles and some snacks for all of them from the kitchen.

"Okay," said Shiva and started towards the roof along with the others.

Sahil had stayed back. "Natasha, I need to talk to you," he said, and Natasha knew that she would have to let the secret out.

Sahil and Natasha joined the others on the rooftop with a couple of bottles of coke and several packets of chips and namkeen, but it was not a rooftop party that they had come to attend, so Sahil took the lead.

"Arjun, Shiva, Ankit, Natasha. Guys you were the closest and best friends of my brother Rahul. In fact, apart from dad and me, you guys formed his second family. And I am glad that even after he is gone, you are fighting to get him justice, no matter the sacrifices that you have being asked to make," said Sahil pointing towards Natasha.

"I am going to discuss something today, and if you guys agree to be a part of it, we would be breaking at least a dozen laws and making some very powerful enemies. We might have to walk looking over our shoulders for the rest of our lives. But if we succeed, we will have ensured that we get justice for Rahul and that no other Rahul has to ever suffer the same fate as my brother did," continued Sahil.

"What do you have in mind, Sahil bhaiya?" asked Shiva.

"How I propose to catch a fish as powerful as Akram is a three pronged strategy: we deceive, we distract and we destroy," thundered Sahil, his fists clenched to form a punch.

Natasha in the meanwhile poured some coke into the plastic glasses that they had brought from the kitchen. They were in for a long night ahead.

"I have been able to lure Akram into believing that I control the Noek's predictions being executed on the trade floor by PAN group traders," continued Sahil picking up a glass that Natasha had just filled and continuing to explain to the group his findings and knowledge about Noek's existence and it's operations.

"Then how did you convince Akram?" said Shiva after listening to everything that Sahil had to say about the Noek.

"Well courtesy his limited knowledge of the existence of the MemoryWall and other defence mechanisms around the Noek, I was able to dupe him into thinking that the Noek has not been empowered enough by its makers to act on its own. And that it just gives out predictions to the operator, and it is the operator, that is me who makes the calls to get the trades executed," said Sahil.

"And did he believe you?"

"Well at first he was sceptical, but then his greed got the better of his judgement, as is the case with most men like him," replied Sahil.

"So we can now pass him any wrong information in the name of the Noek and he would believe us?" This was the next obvious question from Shiva.

Natasha had been unusually quiet the entire time. She seemed lost in her thoughts.

"Well, unfortunately, it is not going to be that simple," said Sahil. "Even if we are able to get Akram to trade on our initial information or suggestions, he will do it rather cautiously the first few times without making any big bets, and if he senses that something is not adding up, it will take him no time to turn on us and come after us."

"So how do we make sure he bets big and loses enough so that he is in no state to come after us?" asked Ankit.

"That's where all of you come in. We will have to work simultaneously and ensure that he bets only once and he loses it all. Natasha has already convinced Mr Sethi to help us in this. He has arranged for a guy who is capable of delaying the live share market feeds to the JONAS offices by a couple of minutes across all platforms, ensuring that we get a window to make Akram trust us with our predictions. So we see the current stock rates and convey it to Akram pretending that they are the Noek's prediction. When Akram sees the same rates across his feeds a couple of minutes later, he will have every reason to believe that our predictions are genuine and can be trusted," said Sahil.

"Whoh! And how did Mr Sethi agree to such a plan, Natasha? I never knew your dad was so cool," interrupted Shiva.

Natasha spoke up for the first time since they had started discussing the plan, completely ignoring Shiva's comment on her dad. "Yes, but this can only work till the point Akram does not decide to act on our information, bhaiya. Once he starts trading on our information, it will not take him much time to analyse his buying reports and realise that the rates we predicted had already been reached by the time we gave the info to him. How do we scrape him off once he makes those trades?"

Things were starting to look interesting and it was already past midnight.

"As far as I know Akram, he will not bet a single rupee in the first few trades that we suggest to him. Not because he would fear risking a small amount of money, but because of his arrogance of being ridiculed and making a fool of himself in his own conscience in case he trusts us and loses even a single paisa. So he would play a wait-and-watch game for the first few trades, which can work to our advantage as we do not want him to trade on our delayed information, but to just gain his trust for the one big trade," Sahil replied.

Sahil had everyone's full attention and continued excitedly, "This is where the guy who is assigned by Natasha's dad will help us. We will be sending across one stock tip to Akram and that guy will ensure that the live feeds to Akram's office remain delayed. We would send him one stock with major upside or downside movement per day for the first three days, which should be enough for him to trust us. We would have deceived him by then."

Everyone else was glued to what he was suggesting. "And during these three days, Shiva and Arjun will have to systematically follow up with Natasha's dad's media and PR contacts and lobby them to leak the news of the existence of Noek into the media at an opportune time. At the end of the third day, the news should be all over print, online and national television."

"Now with such a piece of news in public, SEBI is bound to set up and announce an enquiry committee. This will give us reason to bail your dad's guy and also get Akram to believe that the pressure is mounting on me to cover my tracks and the deal is off. This will serve as our distraction to get him off track and make him desperate to trade on the Noek's predictions."

Sahil was on a roll while all four were listening to him like students listening to a teacher announcing an upcoming exam's question paper.

"Akram having seen the correctness of the initial few trades will not want to let go of the golden hen without making some profit for himself, especially after knowing that it was the same machine that had caused him so many losses in the past. And this is when we will destroy him," Sahil finally concluded.

"Wow bhaiya, sounds like a great plan. But what if he trades in one of the earlier three trades?" asked a concerned Ankit.

"He won't," replied Sahil handing him a burner phone. "Here Ankit, you deliver this burner phone to Akram. This is a phone cum voice transmitter. We will always be aware of what Akram is planning when he is close to this phone. We can improvise if the need arrives."

The Law of the Jungle: Eat or be Eaten

For the strength of the Pack is the Wolf,and the strength of the Wolf is the Pack.

—Rudyard Kipling

3 JULY 2015

Two days later, Natasha received a call from the same blocked number, only this time she had been waiting for it.

"Do you have it?" asked the same voice on the other side of the phone.

"Yes."

"When do you want me to arrange it?" asked the voice.

"It would need to be done on three continuous days. Next Monday 6 July to Wednesday 8 July," replied Natasha, giving him the new plan details.

"What? That was not the plan. I was asked to control the feeds for a few hours at the most," replied the voice clearly surprised.

"Well, it is the plan now. You can ask your boss if he still wants our deal or not," said Natasha in a tone of authority.

"Fine, I will confirm the status by tomorrow. You be ready," replied the voice and disconnected the call.

Natasha was suddenly having an adrenaline rush. It was as though she had tripled the dowry that was being demanded for her being forcefully married. But as far as she knew her father, any demands would have been met at this stage.

5 JULY 2015

Shiva and Arjun were meeting the editor of NEN News at Imperfecto Bar at Cyber Hub in Gurgaon. It was just the first of the many thirty-minute meeting slots that they had arranged with Natasha's contacts at India's top blogs, newspapers and TV channels.

Now the problem with PR is that just like most other good things in life, the people who get it for free are the ones who least need it. Ever looked at that rising star or that overnight hit musician and thought about what they had done so special and so different to get all the media coverage? Well the answer is simpler than you might imagine in most cases – they paid for it. Everyone pays for a good PR, and in some cases like this, even for bad PR of your adversaries.

And after the discovery of his hidden wealth in his own demat bank account, Sahil surprisingly had no shortage of funds for the first time in his life. He had handed over multiple bundles of thousand rupee notes and a file containing all the information that needed to be leaked in the media to Shiva and Arjun. Due to the existence of the safeguards placed by Frank around the Noek, Sahil had to use his imagination in creating the false photo-shopped images along with his real story of the Noek's setup and operations which he had put in the file. And Shiva and Arjun had systematically lined up the money stash with their corresponding files in their bag for each of their scheduled meetings at Imperfecto.

The dark ambience and light music at the Imperfecto Bar made this location ideal for passing the concealed bundles of cash without being noticed and at the same time conveying clearly the date when the message in the file had to be made public.

When the news about the existence of such a machine would get out, the public outcry and pressure itself would be enormous. SEBI would not be able to discard the existence of such an instrument if such a strong proof of its existence was already present in public knowledge.

To uphold public faith in the financial markets and prevent any widespread panic and investor exits, SEBI would have to step in and announce a high level enquiry to investigate the company accused of playing the markets using such an instrument. And in all possibility, to further avoid upsetting the retail investors, Qualified Institutional Investors (QIIs) and Foreign Institutional Investors (FII), it would ban any trades in the stock market by the company accused under the investigation.

Now such an action would surely result in the PAN Group of Companies' stock entering a bottomless downward plunge. And Sahil would have been happy to put the knife through Paul's heart by letting his company's market value collapse, but given the stakes and uncertainties, he could not kill two birds with the same arrow. He could either avenge the murder of his brother or the betrayal of his father. It was an unusual choice, and Sahil had decided that it would have to be the former for the time being.

6 JULY 2015

The bugged burner phone had been delivered to Akram's office by Ankit a couple of days ago and Natasha had been continuously monitoring the audio feeds being received from it. It seemed that Akram had not revealed his secret deal with Sahil to anyone in the office, which was exactly what Sahil had anticipated.

"In order to keep all the praise for himself if the deal goes smoothly and to avoid being seen as a fool if our deal goes south, I suspect Akram would be keeping his little arrangement with me a secret. It will work to our advantage when we bleed him dry," Sahil had said during their meeting at Natasha's rooftop.

So far Sahil had been right on all fronts against Akram, but what worried Natasha was that they were completely in the dark against the PAN Group, whose stock value they would be toying with during the coming week. As far as Natasha knew, it would hit them hard and they'd come back to hurt Sahil for what he was about to do.

It was finally Monday morning. The stage was set, and the big day had arrived. Things were about to get dangerously interesting.

Natasha had already received a message from the blocked number that the two minute delay would be operational on all lines leading to JONAS offices starting Monday 9.30 a.m. for the next three days.

Ankit was in charge of calling Akram and conveying to him the machine's predictions, while Sahil decided to stay on the move, travelling from one part of the city to another in order to keep Paul and his bodyguard distracted from the original scene of action. It was to ensure that the team had no unexpected surprises on PAN's front.

Ankit and Sahil's dad were at their home tracking the day's biggest mover in a two minute time gap. Natasha had decided to join them at Sahil's house to work besides them and keep them updated if she heard anything out of the normal on the audio feed.

Three hours into the market opening bell, and they had their first suggestion, Sparx Technologies had gained 7% in the last two minutes. Ankit who had Akram's burner phone number on speed dial dialled in and blurted out the first of the three suggestions in the upcoming days. Within the next ninety seconds, Akram would know that Sahil meant nothing but business when it came to their arrangement.

As expected, ninety seconds passed and Natasha heard no command from Akram's side to either buy or sell Sparx Tech. He had just asked one of his team members to pull out live feeds for Sparx on the projector screen after he had received Ankit's call. The noise around him suggested he was in a conference room, which meant they all would have watched in awe as the price of Sparx rocketed up within seconds of it being displayed on the projector screen.

On the other side of town, Shiva and Arjun were following up with a different set of their own media contacts with a second bundle of cash and documents. This time with a fatter stash of money and a thinner and different file which Sahil had told them to get through to a separate group of media contacts.

While Natasha was continuously monitoring the audio being received from Akram's burner phone, she was also in touch with Sahil on the current happenings.

She was happy to acknowledge that Sahil had been right once again in predicting their opponent's move. Akram had just observed and not traded on their first tip.

It was turning out to be their day. Shiva had also called up to inform Sahil that their second package had been delivered successfully to the journalists and the journalists had confirmed that it will be leaked to mainstream media only when they would be asked to do the same.

Almost an identical routine took place on Tuesday, when the stock which Mr Kashyap told Ankit to recommend was Asola Metals. Like the previous day, all Akram did was to wait and watch the stock price rise, never ever trying to trade on the stock.

On Wednesday, Sahil asked his dad to increase the number of stocks to three parallel suggestions and decrease the time interval to just sixty seconds so that even if Akram, trusting the authenticity of the tip decided to trade on the suggestions, by the time he decided and got things moving, the stocks would have already reached its target price.

Ankit disclosed the three stocks simultaneously, and by the time Akram had actually decided he would trade for the first time on Sahil's tips, the predicted price was reached on his ticker feeds. He thought he'd have to wait for another day to start making his profits.

That very evening, Sahil, Shiva, Natasha and Arjun made sure that the news of the Noek's existence was flashed on all the sources which had been touched by them.

It was soon to become this country's biggest scandal. PAN Group of Companies' best kept secret was now out in the open.

Short Sold

Injuries are revenged; Crimes avenged.

—Samuel Johnson

"There seems to be some third party involved who would benefit from leaking such information," said Sahil to Akram on the phone before Akram could accuse him of anything.

"What would I gain by leaking the information? I neither have the kind of sources nor the kind of money that is needed to obtain such a coverage. If I had either, I would have been relaxing in a beach house rather than smuggling information for you," justified Sahil.

He had a point and Akram, although reluctant, was fairly convinced. Who knew who all had the Noek caused losses to? Any or all of those people might be in play here.

"So what can we do now?" asked Akram.

"SEBI is a giant of an organisation. It will still take some time for it to act. We can still have at least a couple of trades in which we can make as much money as we want before SEBI decides to launch a full blown enquiry and slay our golden hen," Sahil replied after some thought. "Profits from those trades coupled with the profits that you would have made from my associates' calls in the last three days would be enough for us," Sahil added trying to play with Akram's guilt of not trading on the past few predictions.

"A couple of trades maybe too risky. When SEBI starts the enquiry, they will look into all the abnormally profitable trades that have taken place and all the companies that had benefited from such trades," said Akram. "Now we at JONAS have been making a lot of losses so we may be able to justify one huge out of the blue gain, but two back to back phenomenal gains would be pushing it right onto the SEBI's face and shouting 'investigate us,'" Akram continued.

"And JONAS cannot open itself to a SEBI enquiry. There are a lot of skeletons hiding in our closets. That is the exact reason why we didn't go public about the machine with our information on our own," added Akram before Sahil could suggest otherwise.

"Hmm, you make sense. So maybe one last score that we can pull off using the God's predictions. One score that would settle us and our many generations to come for life," said Sahil with a smile.

The next day, it was Sahil who personally called Akram on his burner phone. This time, he sounded very happy.

"Guess what stock the machine gave out today," said Sahil.

"Be my guest," replied Akram, curiously waiting for the name so that he could make some money.

"Our mutual friend, PAN Group of Companies."

There was a huge smile on Akram's face.

"Strong Sell is the call. Sell as much as you can, Akram. And once you have sold enough, borrow some money and sell some more. It would not take a God to notice how low the PAN's stock prices will go as news about the Noek's existence spreads," said Sahil.

Sahil knew that it was too strong an urge for Akram to resist, and in his emotional state Akram would make his biggest mistake.

"In short, the Noek by suggesting PAN's stock has predicted its own downfall," replied Akram. He could not have been happier.

Sahil had just offered him information with which he would be killing two birds in one stroke – making huge profits for JONAS and at the same time destroying the company which had troubled him and his company for so long.

Akram ordered all his traders to square off all their holdings of whatever stocks they were holding and invest all the money into short selling PAN company stocks. It was a day when the Dalal Street would bleed again, and JONAS would feast.

"Sir," came in Gautam, "we have invested all our funds in short selling PAN shares. Everyone seems to have taken notice and PAN's prices are falling rapidly. It's the herd mentality that has pitched in on the Dalal Street."

"More good news then," replied Akram. "What's our current leverage percentage on PAN's stocks?"

"Sir, it is constant at 50% in accordance with the company's policy of short selling when the trades are not preplanned to be squared off the same day," replied Gautam.

"Hmm, so we have sold just twice the amount of stock than the money we have. That is too less a risk for this sure shot opportunity of a lifetime," said Akram.

"But sir, that is the maximum amount of risk we can take as per the company norms when not day trading," Gautam said with some hesitation.

"I know the company and the policies. Fuck the policies! You don't get your fat bonus checks by following policies to the letter. You get them for making as much money for the company as you can," replied Akram, agitated.

Gautam could do nothing but look on.

"Increase our leverage levels in the market to 10%. Short Sell as much stock of PAN as you can," commanded Akram.

"Sir, but that is less than even the day trading level restrictions," Gautam rebelled.

"Gautam," Akram said after looking at him for a while. "I see myself when I see you - only younger and more aggressive, and ready to take my chair once I leave this company. Don't make me doubt my trust in you by acting so naively."

Gautam had no option left.

JONAS had finally sold Rs. 100 of PAN's stock for every Rs. 10 of the investors' money that the company had in its account. And for forty-four million dollars of investors' money, that was stock worth 440 million dollars short on PAN Group's shares. These were shares that JONAS did not own but had sold anyway, with a promise to buy them at a later time at that time's market price of the PAN stock, price which Akram believed that the Noek had predicted will go down even further.

Akram decided to take the rest of the day off. It was 3.15 p.m. and the markets would close in some time. He, for one last time checked his tickers to see the PAN stock prices continuing its downward spiral.

Considering JONAS had started selling so high, at current prices, JONAS was already standing at 5% profits of its total invested money. Five percent of their leveraged 440 million dollars, which accounted to 22 million dollars, was not bad for a day's earning.

"Tomorrow we will increase these profits tenfold," said Akram to himself as he switched off his screen.

It was seven in the evening and the markets were long closed.

"Shiva," said Sahil over phone, "The time has come for our media friends to leak the contents of that second file. Just in time for today's nine o'clock news."

"Right away," said Shiva and disconnected the phone.

In the meantime, Frank returned to Paul with his report of what he believed was the source of the widespread distribution of news articles and claims about Noek's existence.

It seemed that their new consultant and his friends had been making a lot of out of the way trips to various parts of the city to meet different people. It seemed like a perfect way to pass on classified information in a clandestine way.

Celebrations at Akram's penthouse had begun early. After all, when you are about to make 220 million dollars for your investors in two days' time, your bonus check for that year would read no less than 20 million dollars. Akram's penthouse was flowing with the most expensive liquor and the most exquisite hookers that money could have bought for him in Gurgaon.

It was no fun compared to Vegas, but that would have to wait until weekend when he had squared off his holdings by buying back the shares that he sold short today at throw away prices and then take home those 220 million dollars for JONAS.

There was loud music all around and Akram was so drunk that he was having trouble fucking even one of the many hookers that surrounded him. There was no way he could have noticed Gautam's seventeen missed calls and fifteen messages – all saying the same thing in different words –

Are you watching the news?

Turn on CNBC.

Pick Up.
Are you alive?
Where the fuck are you??!!!
We are screwed!!

NEXT DAY

It was 7.30 a.m. and Akram woke up from the stench of the puke all around him. He must have had one too many drinks yesterday. His head was bursting with pain.

"Oh God, what a night!" he said to himself as he got out of the shower and made himself a cup of black coffee.

He sat down on the only uncluttered part of the sofa that he could find and called the guard to bring in the newspapers over the penthouse service intercom.

"Were you the one on duty last night?" he asked the guard as he knocked and entered the dining area.

"Yes," replied the guard.

"What happened?" Akram asked.

"Sir, the madams left around three in the morning and you were pretty drunk when you came out to drop them. So as per your instructions to the supervisor, he sent me to escort you back in. I made you lay down on the sofa and then left after putting the door on auto lock," replied the guard earnestly.

"Good and thank you. Now hand me those newspapers and you don't talk about this to anyone," said Akram handing the guard a five hundred rupee note and dismissing him with a wave of his hand.

Akram must have thought that it was still his hangover that was making him hallucinate when he picked up the *Financial*

Times and read the headlines:

PAN Group's quarterly earnings estimated to be up by more than 100%. Dividend may be announced for the first time in the company's history

News Reporter, July 10, 2015

After a bad day at stock markets on Thursday, late evening news reports of PAN Group's earnings of the previous April –
June quarter put the fears of the company's stock price plunge on account of a SEBI enquiry to rest. The SEBI enquiry, whose announcement at a probable future date is being said to be nothing more than a formality, is being demanded on the basis of some wild allegations that the PAN Group possesses some super human machine with alien technology of reading and predicting the stock market's future.

Continued on Page 4

Akram rushed to find his phone only to find Gautam's thirty-one missed calls and forty-three messages and finally one e-mail. Akram opened the e-mail sent by Gautam at 1.15 a.m which was addressed to him and cc'd to the entire company…

We are screwed. Courtesy our high leverage, we will have lost all of our investors' money within one minute of markets' opening tomorrow morning. There will be no sellers in the market for the PAN stock, only buyers, and we could not buy at that price even if we wanted to. The predictions are that the PAN stock would open on a

15% premium tomorrow morning, enough to wipe us out completely considering our current 5% profits on the stock and Akram's decision to raise our leverage to 10% against all predefined rules.

Please consider this my resignation.

Gautam

Akram looked at his watch. It was 8.30 a.m., just one hour between his yesterday's profits of 22 million in one day turning into a total loss of 44 million dollars in one night. And there was nothing he could do but watch.

The Greatest Fool

Forgiveness is a gift you give to yourself.

—Suzanne Somers

At the Pacific Mall in West Delhi, it was the usual hustle bustle of a regular Friday evening.

Paul was waiting for Sahil at the corner-most table of the food court while Frank stood beside him keeping a close guard on any eminent threat in such an open setting.

"Congratulations, Mr Kashyap," spoke Paul, his voice heavy with the lack of sleep as Sahil got off from the escalators and approached Paul's table.

"I am not sure what you mean Paul," Sahil replied, deciding to behave naively.

"Well, I just congratulated you on successfully playing the greatest 'Greater Fool Game' ever," Paul reiterated.

"Well Paul, I am still not sure what you mean, but whatever it is, I would like to thank you for inviting me here," said Sahil, trying to play along as Paul deliberately stayed silent, as if waiting for Sahil to speak up.

Sahil was getting more and more uncomfortable by each passing second as he sat in front of Paul. He was constantly being stared at by Frank. Sahil was repeatedly thinking to himself whether he had willingly walked himself into a death trap, and whether there were some snipers waiting to pull the trigger as soon as Paul indicated. He wondered whether there was some assassin waiting outside the mall to take him out in a road accident just like his brother. The worst part of such a road kill would have been that Sahil had no brother left to avenge his murder.

"But I came here to personally inform you that I would like to quit from the job of the consultant," Sahil said, trying to digress from the topic.

Sahil had thought to himself that Paul could never, under any circumstances, know about him quitting the job until Sahil had actually disappeared and gone into hiding. The odd gaps of silence, however, had forced Sahil to unwillingly cough up the topic.

"Well, I hope you know, Mr Kashyap, that these are not the type of decisions that you can take on your own and *inform* us later as you pass by," said Paul, laying great emphasis on the word 'inform'.

"Yes I know, and I am sorry for not keeping you in the loop, but some things have come up and I will no longer be able to continue serving the Noek."

"If you say so Mr Kashyap," said Paul in a much calmer tone this time. "I hereby accept your resignation effective this moment on account of your inability to serve as the second operator cum consultant."

Sahil closed his eyes, as if waiting to be shot by the imaginary sniper's bullet. This had to be it. The indication that Paul had to give to his shooter to make Paul's words come true would be-*'on account of your inability to serve as the second operator'*, Sahil was sure. The only thought in his head was why did he even agree to come here to meet Paul.

A minute passed, and then another, and yet Sahil felt nothing. Was he dead already or was it that Paul had decided to kill him in a road accident instead.

"Open your eyes, Mr Kashyap. I don't execute my ex-employees in public places," said Paul.

"Well you should kill me while you still have a chance, Paul," uttered Sahil, not knowing why he did so. Sahil assumed it was the fear of inevitable death that had made him fearless in front of his executors.

"Well, more than the fact that I respect your father for keeping the Noek's secret for almost three decades, I admire your courage of doing what you did for your younger brother. Even more so, I admire your finesse in executing the greatest 'Greater Fool Theory' I have seen in my life," said Paul, making it clear that he was not letting go of the topic until Sahil had confessed to what he had done.

Sahil decided it was no use trying to evade the topic and thus he decided to take it head on, "And what is it Paul? The thing that you repeatedly refer to as the greatest execution of the greatest fool?"

"I have seen people sell worthless startups to others at hundred times its value, and I have seen people buy real estate at enormous prices on the assumption that they will be able to sell it off later to a greater fool than themselves for an even higher price. But I have not in my life, ever, ever seen someone sell information on a dysfunctional machine to a seasoned investor like Akram, who headed one of India's most fierce financial companies, and make it worth his millions," said Paul in a very animated voice.

"You have indeed pulled off the bravest stunt in this century's financial history, but sadly for you boy, you played this game with someone else's money. My money, and that makes me wonder whether your bravest stunt would also prove to be your most foolish decision," continued Paul.

"Well if it provides you any solace, Paul, your machine or my dad's machine, the great Noek was rendered useless by this same seasoned investor whom I destroyed using your name and money.

The Noek was left dysfunctional by Akram's team using bots to clutter and manipulate its input because it was learning and then causing JONAS's traders to lose a lot more money courtesy their risk taking strategies and leveraging," said Sahil.

Sahil spoke as if this was his last time. "In this great ocean where small fish always ends up being eaten by a bigger fish, the only way for me to beat a shark like Akram was to use your company's name and fame to create a façade of power around the shark. An illusion of power and revenge that was too great even for a man like Akram to ignore. He eventually let his greed take the bait and ended up being eaten instead.

"You owe my dad more than two decades of his life and his work that you stole from him. Something that all your money combined cannot pay for, and I just made a dent in your fortunes, Paul. Consider it a 99% off sale. I exposed the secret that my dad had kept for decades. You can take it as my dad's resignation from holding on to your secret."

Paul had been patiently listening to what Sahil had to say. It was as though he was granting Sahil his last wish – the right to free speech, and when Sahil eventually finished, Paul had a couple of things to say.

Paul spoke, "I accept your and your father's resignation, boy. You may leave now. And yes, do give your father my best regards. We had some great time during our college days."

Sahil quietly stood up, dead sure that he would not be alive when his dad saw him next, but at least he had made a dent in Paul's pride, after making a dent in his fortune. This is as close as anyone gets to hurting a whale like Paul, thought Sahil to himself while leaving the food court.

"Where do you want me to do it?" Frank asked Paul as Sahil walked away.

"Not today, Frank. Not today. Let the boy go," replied Paul. "I have owed his father for his silence and for his half of this company's wealth long enough. It is only justified that his son wanted to settle this debt by only making a dent in what he otherwise would have inherited. Consider this my payback."

Frank put his revolver back into its sleeve.

Zero Sum Game

What goes around, comes around.

—Karma

It was already being labelled as the big fat Indian wedding of the season. After all, it is not every day that you get to see the DG of Telecom's only daughter marrying the only son of the Indian Ambassador to Switzerland, Mr. Sandeep Gambhir. The who's who of the Indian political circle had been invited to the destination wedding being held at the Neemrana Palace. The magnificent fort had been truly fortified for the entire week of celebrations.

Natasha had not invited any of her friends from college except Shiva, Ankit and Arjun. Sahil and Mr Kashyap were also on the invitees list, but Natasha knew they wouldn't come. She had already received the bouquet Sahil had sent for her. So apart from the three musketeers from her college, the only people she knew at this carnival of a wedding were her relatives, family friends and their cousins, and their cousins' cousins and so on. After all, no one wanted to not be on the invitees list.

Although Natasha was fond of dancing and going wild at any chance she could garner, she had seemed rather indifferent in the five days, since all of them had arrived at the palace. It was as if she had left the child within her back in Delhi, or maybe she had strangled that child when she had agreed to marry a total stranger against her will.

Either way, she was not sure what was a more liberating thought for her? That she would not have to stay in India any more, at a place which would remind her of Rahul every day after her marriage, or that she had succeeded in getting justice for the person whom she had loved more than anyone else in her entire life.

Natasha was all ready to go to the mandap when her mom entered her room. Natasha was looking stunning in her golden orange designer lehenga. Mrs Sethi had selected the design over the internet and then got it made by one of the most famous designers in Mumbai. The fact that the lehnga cost more than twenty lakhs added to its elegance. Had Rahul been here, he could not have stopped staring, Natasha thought to herself while being accompanied by Mrs Sethi to the mandap.

On her way, her three musketeers joined Mrs Sethi to escort Natasha. Once they reached the mandap, Shiva hugged Natasha and whispered in her ears, "We know why you agreed to this marriage. Sahil bhaiya told us everything. We want to let you know that you would always remain the girl who Rahul wanted to see happy. If you ever need us, don't hesitate to ask, bhabhi."

Natasha was not going to wipe off the tear that had rolled down her left cheek.

"Your name, sir?" asked the officer.

"Vijay Kashyap," answered Vijay.

"And your purpose of visit – business or pleasure?" enquired the officer again.

"The pleasure of doing business," replied Vijay, not sure whether the officer understood what he meant, but it no longer mattered. They were in a country with no extradition to India for the crimes that they had committed.

On their way out of the Fiji Islands International Airport, Sahil pointed towards the cab that was waiting for them next to the huge airport entry sign. The father-son duo boarded the cab with their luggage and headed off for their guesthouse.

Sahil looked at his wrist watch which was still set to Indian time and realised it was the approximate time that Natasha would be taking her sacred vows. A thought of calling the courier company to confirm the delivery of the bouquet that he had sent for Natasha's marriage crossed Sahil's mind, but he decided against it. He also thought back on the messages he had left for Shiva, Ankit and Arjun.

Fiji was a magical place. Apart from it being a tax haven, it was a country with no extradition treaties with any of the eastern countries. This implied that Sahil and his dad could roam freely on its streets and enjoy its scenic beauty without the fear of being hunted down by the cops for what they had done in the past. Also, it was nearly halfway around the world for either Akram or Paul to track them. With Sahil making sure that no one knew where they were going, what were the chances of either of Akram or Paul coming to Fiji on a vacation and spotting Sahil there?

But apart from all this, what got Vijay interested the most was the fact that he could start trading in any of the world's developing markets from here without any bans or restrictions to slow him down. The pleasure of doing business, as he had rightly told the officer at the airport.

The cab dropped them off at their guest house, or guest palace, as Sahil named it later. It was more of a sprawling villa just for the two of them. When Sahil was making the bookings for the first week of their stay, he never knew money could be such a facilitator.

The beach house or the villa had a huge curved viewing cum dining room facing the ocean, with the steps out of the room leading to a six feet deep and eighteen feet wide swimming pool. The porch had two comfortably cushioned beach chairs with a mini bar in between them. As soon as Vijay entered the dining room and lay his eyes on the beach chairs, he could already visualise him making his next million rupees' trading, sitting on those chairs. Or would it now be his next million dollars, considering they had gone international and Vijay was already eyeing the nascent African stock exchanges.

"Dad, this is too exquisite," said Sahil, still trying to take in the beauty of the place.

"Yes it is, my boy, which is why I have just decided to buy it," replied his dad.

"Dad, jokes apart, I agree you have been able to get our money out of India using your ways, but coming to think of it, we weren't left with much, if you take into account how much money we spent on buying the press and then gifting to Shiva, Ankit and Arjun," argued Sahil earnestly.

"Well, if you consider the initial crores that you had seen in your account, I agree we haven't left ourselves with much taking into account the twenty percent hawala I paid to get our money transferred to Fiji," replied Sahil's dad with a naughty smile.

"But, if you take into account the ninety crores that I made in one day by day trading the PAN group stock when you leaked their fake earnings in the media, well, I would say we have plenty to last us a lifetime, buy us this Villa and a Ferrari!"

"What?" shouted Sahil in total disbelief. "You bet our entire savings on the successful dissemination of our fake earnings report?"

"Well, that is one way to put it. The other way to say this is that I risked everything and I made us ninety crore rupees in the span of six hours, leading to an earning rate of fifteen crore rupees per hour," replied Vijay, remembering his first discussion with Paul during Professor Subramaniam's lecture almost three decades ago when he set out to design the Noek.

"Dad, that is not the point here. My point is you gave in to your addiction of gambling while we all were fighting with Akram as well as Paul," argued Sahil.

"Old habits die hard, my son, especially when you have a decades-old nemesis to annihilate in front of you."

Akram was finally summoned for the board meeting. He had been waiting for the call since the past half hour, but supposedly the board of directors, considering his past record, had seemed divided on their final decision regarding Akram.

"May I come in, sir?" requested Akram softly.

"Yes, please have a seat," replied one of the seven board members with the yellow tie, seated at the farthest side of the conference table facing Akram.

"Would you like to have anything, tea or coffee?" asked another board member.

"I am sure Mr Sabharwal that Mr Akram would have had tea or coffee before coming if he needed one, considering he has been running this office for the past so many years," interrupted the same director with the yellow tie.

The mood seemed hostile, but there was nothing Akram could have done to change it, considering he had lost more than 250 crore rupees of investors' money in a single day of trading. And not just that, he had in the process of doing so, flouted all the set margin safety requirements that are religious to a trading company like JONAS.

The fact that such an error came from a guy who had been running the company for the last fifteen years only added up to the seriousness of the crime, instead of acting as a pacifier of the same.

"Mr Akram, we would like to inform you that the board has reached a consensus in your case of ignorance of all the rules and regulations sacred to this organisation, and that you in your full conscience wilfully proceeded with such an act raises questions over the morality and righteousness of your fifteen years of service to this organisation."

"Sir, with all due respect, it was me who drafted all these rules that you refer to today and it was me who helped this company grow and made it into an organisation by initiating new sources of potential income, including the day-trading department whose regulations you are referring to," Akram had no idea what he was blabbering and he was hardly able to hold back his tears while speaking when he was interrupted by another board member.

"Enough," shouted the member sitting closest to Akram at the conference table.

"So, as I was saying, taking into account all of what you just mentioned and your fifteen years of service to this company turned organisation courtesy you, Mr Akram, we, the board of directors have come to a consensus that you are to be terminated from the services of JONAS Partners effective immediately. You will be escorted out of the office by one of the security guards and your personal belongings in the office, if any, will be shipped to you after thorough investigation," continued the director with the yellow tie, reading form the file in front of him.

"The majority shareholders using their special power assigned to them in the company's founding articles, hereby strip you of any stock options and employee retirement benefits that you might have been eligible for. You are, however, free to challenge this decision in the court of law on your own expenses," the director continued reading.

"With all due respect sir," interrupted Akram, "I know my way out. It was an honour serving this organisation. You can send the rest of your decision with my personal belongings. I accept my termination," continued Akram while getting up from his chair and leaving the room. A security guard followed Akram through the corridor to the exit gate and then the lifts to make sure that Akram would not return to the office premises.

The whole office observed in silence and shock as the person they had looked upon as the face of the organisation walked through the corridor for one last time. He was in tears and accompanied by a security guard, as if he was some kind of a prisoner. Most of them had only heard rumours of what had happened after they had received Gautam's resignation email, while others had wondered who was next on the list of terminations. A selected few were delighted that they might finally get a chance to have a go at the chair that had been so closely guarded by Akram for the past several years.

Shreya had brought in another box full of framed images while Mukul was still struggling to figure out places to drill holes for the previous box of frames.

"Here's another and the last of them," said Shreya.

"Shreya, sweetheart, you realise we are already short of space," said Mukul in a very soothing voice.

"So what," replied Shreya, "we can always move to the next wall."

"Well, not exactly. This is the last of the walls left, and there is no way I can hang up all of these frames without making the walls of our new office look like a collage of random images," replied Mukul.

"A collage seems like a good idea to attract new clients to our start-up," joked Shreya.

"Yeah, of course, and while we are at it, let us have a mascot of a baby elephant outside our office distributing pamphlets," teased Mukul.

"That would be so cute! We should definitely try it out," she said chuckling.

"Yeah exactly, and risk our clients perceiving us as a baby day care centre instead of stock market consultants!"

"Mukul, you are a genius. No wonder you married me. That is such a good idea. Let us provide free future day care for the toddlers of our newly-married clients who hire us as their stock market consultants," said Shreya, her eyes lighting up with excitement.

"Anything you say, my angel. Now help me get this board up," replied Mukul holding up the board that read:

SM Consultants Private Limited

Although most of their middle-aged clients were told that the name stood for *Stock Market Consultants Private Limited*, a few of their newly-wed clients knew that the firm which was handling their assets was called *Shreya & Mukul Consultants Private Limited.*

On his way home, Shiva thought it would be better to go to a doctor and get some medicine for his sore throat, given the pounding that his throat had taken in the past seven days during the carnival wedding.

"How was the wedding beta?" asked Shiva's mom when he entered his flat in Janakpuri, a locality situated in West Delhi.

"It was wonderful Mom, but please don't expect me to get married anytime soon. I have to earn a lot of money before that," he replied from the washroom.

"Oh c'mon, you are earning well enough. You can easily support a wife with twenty thousand rupees. Your dad used to do it with much less," she shouted from the kitchen.

"Ya whatever," shouted Shiva as he walked out of the washroom and into his room.

"Mom, whose duffel bag have you kept on in my almirah, and what's in it?" shouted Shiva as he saw the bag.

"Oh that... Rahul's brother Sahil came over a day after you all had left for Natasha's wedding. He said it had some stuff of yours and asked me to give it to you when you got back. I told him to keep it in your room. He must have put it into your almirah," shouted Shiva's mom over the whistle of the pressure cooker in the kitchen.

"My stuff?" Shiva wondered to himself as he opened the bag.

To his amazement, the bag was filled with bundles of thousand rupee notes and had a letter on top of the cash that read:

Dear Shiva,

Thank you for everything you did for Rahul in the past few months. Rahul was indeed a lucky man to have friends like you three. It was sad that he, like my dad, trusted the wrong guys when it came to money.

While we fly away from our past and all the charges that SEBI and others might levy on us, I cannot help but think of whether there is anything I can do to prevent what happened to Rahul from happening to any of you.

The bag contains some money that might come in handy as you pass through the highs and lows of your life. Use it wisely.

Stay happy, stay safe.

Love

Sahil

Shiva was left standing stupefied.

"Your phone has been ringing for the past few minutes, pick it up!" Shiva's mom said while passing his room.

Shiva returned to his senses. It was Arjun calling. As soon as Shiva picked up his call, he was bombarded by a super elated Arjun.

"Did you get the..."

"Yes," replied Shiva, looking at the bag one more time.

"Did you read..." asked Arjun.

"Yes," replied Shiva smiling.

"Did you count..." asked Shiva finally as Arjun paused for a second to breathe for the first time since he called.

"Yes," replied Arjun.

"How much is there?" asked Shiva.

"Exactly the same amount as Rahul had asked us for that night... Five Crores," replied Arjun.

A personal note from the author

Hi guys! I hope you liked my first work of fiction. Just wanted to thank you all for your support. Do recommend this book to your friends and colleagues if you liked it. If you have suggestions for my next book, please get in touch with me on pulkit@cabsguru.com and I will surely get back to you. Also it would be a matter of great happiness for me to give away pre-order copies of my next book to the best feedbacks.

While Sahil's father is still busy printing money out of his passion and addiction for beating the stock markets, a new exciting journey is about to begin soon.

Till next time... thank you all.

Endnotes

[1] For those of us wondering about what is a Second Round of Funding, Here's a playful insight...
Now, no matter how difficult or complex the investment decisions and logics behind the investment of millions and millions of dollars in a particular company at a particular time are, the good guys in the financial domain always believe in keeping it simple for the outside world.

For example, say if a company is funded to start its operations, it is said to have been seed funded. Similarly, a new round of funding after seed funding is called, well simply. "First round of funding" and the same is followed by a second round and then a third round until the company decides it has grown enough to come out with an IPO, in which the general public can invest money in a private company which is going public.

Well for those of us who are wondering why a company needs so many rounds, it is typically because the earlier investors need avenues to exit and book their profits while newer investors feel the greed to join the growing company's bandwagon. And also, the often overlooked fact, these several rounds of funding provide the wheels of the Greater Fool Theory to spin and take their course.

[2] B-Plan or Business Plan
A Business Plan or a B-Plan in short is a formal statement of business goals, plans about how they are attainable, and plans for reaching them. It may

also contain background information about the organization or team attempting to reach those goals. (Source: Wikipedia)
You can read more about B-Plans and its components on Wikipedia - http://en.wikipedia.org/wiki/Business_plan
B-Plans are generally the first serious step towards converting your idea into a full-fledged business.

(3) Greater Fool Theory ? ? !
As I mentioned earlier, in the field of finance, the theory names do mostly end up implying what they are actually meant to suggest. Similarly in this case, the famous Greater Fool Theory suggests nothing but typical investor behaviour in which one investor buys an asset at a price much higher than its actual intrinsic value in the hope that he could sell his investment at an even higher price to another investor (who in this case is a greater fool than the first investor) after a certain period of time.

The beauty of the Greater Fool Theory is that it is applicable in almost all domains of financial transactions, involving asset valuation - be it the mango public when it comes to Real Estate (typical buying of baselessly highly priced flats or land, holding and then reselling of the same property at even higher prices), or be it professional analysts when it came to investment in other companies - multimillion dollar investments in companies with scintillating business plans on paper and zero profits on the ground.

In the history of financial markets, all such investments that were made on behalf of the greater fool paradigm have usually led to is the creation of asset bubbles, which eventually busted when the investor fear of losing money overpowered their greed of earning more money from a particular investment, leading to an eventual crash in the market prices.